HOT ROD HISTORY

BOOK TWO: THE GLORY YEARS

BY TOM MEDLEY

TRACING AMERICA'S MOST POPULAR AUTOMOTIVE HOBBY

Printed and bound in the United States of America

FIRST PRINTED IN 1994 BY CO-PUBLISHERS:

CARTECH, INC., 11481 Kost Dam Road, North Branch, MN 55056
and
TEX SMITH PUBLISHING, P.O. Box 726, Driggs, ID 83422

COPYRIGHT BY TOM MEDLEY 1994

CARTECH, INC. and TEX SMITH PUBLISHING COMPANY
recommend you follow all safety procedures when working on your vehicle.
Wear eye protection and respiration filter, especially when painting and around tools.
Always dispose of hazardous fluids, batteries, tires and parts properly
and safely to protect our environment.

CARTECH, INC., and TEX SMITH PUBLISHING COMPANY books are also available at discounts in bulk quantity for industrial or sales-promotional use. For details, contact the marketing director at:
CARTECH, INC., 11481 Kost Dam Road, North Branch, MN 55056
Telephone (612) 583-3471, FAX (612) 583-2023

OVERSEAS DISTRIBUTION BY:

BROOKLANDS BOOKS LTD.
P.O. Box 146, Cobham, Surrey, KT11 1LG, England
Telephone 0932 865051, FAX 0932 868803

BROOKLANDS BOOKS LTD.
1/81 Darley Street, P.O. Box 199, Mona Vale, NSW 2103, Australia
Telephone 2 997 8428, FAX 2 452 4679

ISBN 1-884089-08-9

Printed and bound in the United States of America.

AUTHOR	TOM MEDLEY
PUBLISHER	LEROI TEX SMITH
EDITOR	BRIAN BRENNAN
TECH. EDITOR	RON CERIDONO
ART DIRECTOR	GREG COMPTON
ART ASSISTANT	LISA HANKS

CONTENTS

FOREWORD

This is the second book in our Tom Medley *Hot Rod History* series. We pick up here where we left off with Book One, and you'll note that we go from before World War II well into the Street Rod era. Some have called this the Golden Age of the automobile, quite debatable to those of us who always look forward to setting a new speed record, rather than resting on a record set years ago. Whether there will be more from Tom Medley depends. It depends on whether or not Tom wants to put one together, and whether or not we want to publish one, and whether or not there is enough of a market out there in hot rod land.

There are quite a few hot rod histories beginning to surface, some very good, some marginal. Some, such as our own newly finished *Roaring Roadsters,* a track roadster history by Don Radbruch, are unique and alone in the field. The Tex Smith Hot Rod History books are different, in that we like to do first person accounts as much as possible. For most of us who are considered gray beards in the sport, we don't really think of it as history... just something interesting that happened before our bodies and minds became so, well, seasoned.

Because these are generally first person accounts, the photos are usually simple snapshots as well, from personal archives. They aren't professional, they simply help tell the hot rod story from an individual's own perspective. We even keep editing to a minimum, because we want the flavor of the individual's character to come across. In hot rodding, especially in any of the highly competitive aspects of the sport, there are no wimps. What you see is what you get! Which in most cases is far more than a handful.

I've been fortunate to know virtually all of the people in these histories. Too often these days, I get word of someone passing away, someone who will always seem ageless, an active and vibrant young person. For me, each represents a milestone in automotive history, and each should be in a hot rod hall of fame. Few will be, perhaps, since popular historians are prone to rely too heavily on media and too little on contemporaries. Trust me on this, though, all the people that we have spotlighted in our books, and most of those in other hot rod histories, were doers. They didn't sit around and wait for things to happen, they went out and made things happen. Which is, in the long run, the very essence of hot rodding.

If you don't have Tom Medley's *Hot Rod History, Book One,* give us a call and get one now. Same with *Roaring Roadsters,* same with all the available hot rod history books. Someday, they won't be in print, and you will have missed a major chunk of the golden era of the automobile. Isn't it great that hot rodding is now old enough, and respected enough, to have a history?

For the whole story on track roadster racing, see Tex Smith's *Roaring Roadsters*

CHUCK ABBOTT

I met Chuck "Red" Abbott right after the war when I moved to Glendale to go to the Art Center. We used to hang out at Parker's Night Owl, that's where all the action was with the roadsters. The first time I talked a lot with Chuck was at a Sidewinder club meeting at Kong Jackson's place in Glendale. Over the years he's been a dyed in the wool hot rodder. For ever and ever he's been at the lakes and Bonneville, in fact he and Kong Jackson went to Bonneville in his '29 roadster just to see Cobb and watch the Novi run. That's a pretty long trip, you gotta be hardcore to do that. Over the years, I've run into him working on the HOT ROD MAGAZINE Special, working at the Speedway on the Novi, etc. He's always been around racing, been on crew, worked for Bill Stroppe, always been around race cars no matter what. Great guy to talk to about the old days because he's got a lot of good tales to tell. He's retired from the phone company now. He still gets around to all the affairs, I've seen him at the Throttlers picnic in just about anything that moves. Any tales he's told or pictures he's provided for this book are the real McCoy. No baloney, always the straight stuff and always looking for a way to help others, what I consider a thoroughbred hot rodder.

TOM: When did you get interested in this hot rod stuff?

CHUCK: I was about 14 years old I guess. There was this neighbor by the name of Paul Simon, and he was a friend of Paul Werk and Art Sparks, they had this SR Fronty.

TOM: What year was this?

CHUCK: This was about '35 or '36. This Fronty was a Model T, had a two-port intake and three-port exhaust, and it was going down the street with just some straight stacks sticking out. I thought, boy, that's for me. Had a regular side drive mag on it, and a big 97 painted on the side of it because that's how fast they'd run up at Muroc. Couple other friends of mine and I decided that was for us. We found a Model T for a dollar, and a battery for a dollar, and we all pushed it home.

TOM: Where'd you buy it?

CHUCK: Somebody had it all torn apart and they

Yam Okas' sharp-looking '32 looks even better in this shot from the timing stand taken at an El Mirage, 1947 meet. Chuck Abbott is the handler.

never got it back together. So we went down to the library and got a *Dyke's Automotive Encyclopedia.* It told all about how to hot rod a Model T. How to drill holes in the rods, about Ryolite pistons, anyhow we finally got it running. It probably took about a year, we got it up to the lakes and ran 101 mph.

TOM: Who drove it?

CHUCK: George Normington, I didn't want to drive it, I'd rather work on it. That was at Muroc, 1937 or '38.

TOM: That was about the Purdy brothers era wasn't it?

CHUCK: That was Purdy brothers, who did the timing. I got to help time our car. Sat in Duke Hallock's big dump truck with the timing device up in the dump bed. Then the wind came up, and it got so dusty that everybody packed up and went home. That's where I ran into Harry Oka and Pat Kapia. They had a four-port Riley that ran 120 mph, and Rufi's three-port Chevy Modified. That was before the streamliners. They ran 120 mph.

TOM: Did you have a car in high school?

CHUCK: No, after high school. I didn't have any money in high school. First car I had after the model T, one of the other partners and I bought a two cam Fronty, but it was all cracked, the head was no good so that never materialized. Then I bought a Cragar, a '30 roadster with a Model B engine. I got too many tickets with it, my dad frowned on that. So I traded the '30 for a real terrible looking '29 roadster pickup. I never had any more trouble getting tickets, because they never bothered looking at that old piece of junk.

TOM: Remember when you were running the Thingee?

Twenty members of the Glendale Sidewinders were on hand for this 1947 club meeting picture. It could be 21 members if the cameraman was also a member.

CHUCK: Doug Gregory was the starter, A. Needus used to take home all the money. Lou Senter, too. Wheeler dealers.

TOM: Tell me about the trip you went on in Kong's roadster.

CHUCK: That was in 1948. We knew Bud Winfield pretty good, and they had the Novi that Ab Jenkins was gonna run at Bonneville for 12 hour and 24 hour overall speed records. They had a 10 mile circle laid out, so I took my vacation. I was working for Western Electric, and we decided we were gonna go and watch the Novi run. We got up there and they had burned a rod. We went up in Jackson's '29 roadster on a '32 frame, with a three-eighths flathead. I don't think we ever went under. It was so cold, and this was in August, I figured we couldn't get there too quick.

The methanol fuel they were using for the race car, they had to take it from one 50-gallon drum to another, through a chamois skin to get all the water out of it. You can really get a headache breathing that

stuff. It was terrible. Cobb was up there at that time, with a Railton. It was built before the war. General Petroleum was sponsoring them, they were also sponsoring Bud Winfield. GP was the flying red horse. Every afternoon those Englishmen would stop and have their tea, it didn't matter what. And Winfield, he'd really get on them, because they weren't using flush rivets and they didn't have the wheels faired in, and here they were running almost 400 mph, when it ran. The carbs still had cork floats in them.

TOM: What were they using for engines?

CHUCK: I think they were the H 24 Napier. They were big. Great big tires also. Dunlop tires on it. They were true British all the way.

TOM: Who drove the Novi?

CHUCK: Ab Jenkins drove it part of the time, they finally decided, they got desperate at the end there,

Seated, Fred Huber and Kong Jackson (behind wheel), with Major Gilbert holding up the windshield.

Bonneville Salt Flats 1947. The Novi Indy car complete with enclosed canopy was on hand to do some running on a giant circle course. Ab Jenkins was to drive, but his son Marv did most of the driving. The '29 A-V8 roadster belonged to Chuck Abbott. He and Kong Jackson drove it all the way from Glendale to Wendover just to see not only the Novi run but also John Cobb's streamliner run. They were the first SCTA members ever to run their car on the salt.

they spent all this money and time up there, they were gonna do something. Lou Welsh got in it, and went out and ran a straight-away to get some kind of a record. I think he did get some kind of an American, not a world record. I think Class C right around 220 mph.

Balsh had his midget up there at that time, and the best they could get out of that midget was 140 mph, no matter what they did. Up and down, up and down, no matter what they did, 140. Change tires, up and down, still 140mph. I said it wouldn't hurt to try some dirt tires.

On the way home with Kong Jackson, we stopped in Palmdale. We needed gas, and I thought he still had some money. We go in and have lunch, I paid for the lunch, and come out to get gas, and he has no money. He'd spent it all at the crap table back at Wendover. Luckily, one of the AAA officials, I can't remember his name,

A mechanic works on the Cobb Land Speed 'liner in the Mobile station in downtown Wendover, Utah, 1947. The Cobb car was powered with a Napier Saber World War I aircraft engine. It ran no radiator, but used ice to cool the engine. Cobb ran 403 mph one way, with a two-way average of 396 mph. Power was to all four wheels.

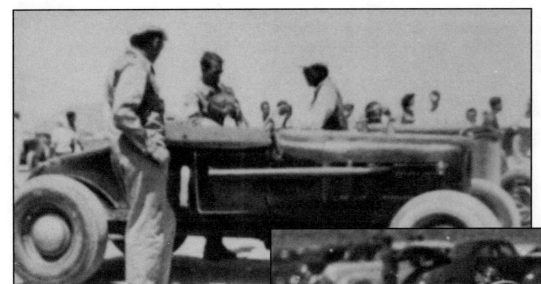

The unusually long hood on this '27 T roadster must house an interesting power plant.
No information available on this car.

Chuck Abbott, Glendale, California, moves out in Yam Oka's '32 roadster, El Mirage dry lake bed.

came in, and he loaned us five bucks. We had enough to get gas and another hamburger.

That trip to Bonneville was how I got to know Jean Marsinac real well. From then on I started goin' over to his shop in my spare time, and help on the Novi. Then after Bud Winfield was killed, they moved from Glendale to Burbank.

TOM: What happened to Bud?

CHUCK: He was killed in an automobile accident up by Fresno. Walt James, I can't remember who was driving the car, some guy came out of a side street, ran a stop sign and hit them broadside, right in the back seat where Bud Winfield was sitting. 1955 or so.

TOM: Did you know Bob Stelling?

CHUCK: Yeah, I knew him before the war.

TOM: When did you go to the speedway?

CHUCK: 1952 was the first time I went to Indy. I'd worked on the Novi enough that I had to go back and see it run. There were two cars, Chet Miller drove one of them, Duke Nalon drove the other. I never will forget, I don't care what, first day of qualifying, we drove that Novi out and I couldn't figure what all the people were whooping about. There were over 100,000 people in the grandstands, the place was

packed, a beautiful day, and all of a sudden everybody goes crazy. I asked Jean, what the hell's going on? He said it was all for the Novi race car. Anybody else could push a car out and it didn't make any difference. That place went crazy. I think Chet Miller went out first. That reception for the Novi impressed me more than anything else back there.

TOM: I remember how they would come down that chute, and it would echo in between those old stands, it sounded so much different than anything else. Make the hair stand up on the back of your neck. Lotsa horsepower. Especially compared to everyone else.

CHUCK: They were sure a drawing card. A real major league drawing card. I sure met a lot of nice people back there. I went back with the Novi again in 1955.

TOM: When did Rutman drive?

CHUCK: In '54-'55. He didn't qualify, so I came home, in fact that was the year that Vuki got killed. I went back again in '57. I was working for Western

Electric as a supervisor, and my boss knew I was interested in Indianapolis, got him to send me to the supervisor's training school at the Tradeland Plant in Indiana. All those four weeks I'd go down to the speedway every night and clean out the garage, and get it all ready. This was in April so I spent all of April and May back there. It was quite an education. Some of the guys I knew were already living there.

TOM: Who designed that Novi engine to begin with?

CHUCK: Bud did, Bud and Leo. More a combination of several people, but basically Bud's idea.

TOM: They had trouble with the air cooler and blower drives shearing, didn't they?

CHUCK: One year both cars went out with the shafts broken. Chet Miller and Duke, both. They should've won that thing. I wasn't back there that one year. When they fueled the tank, it backed up out of the hole, with the Novi leading the race. I think Duke was driving. They thought the tank was full getting close to the end of the race. They ended up third because they were running out of gas. With a new fueling system, they then could put in 115 gallons in nine-and-

One of many bobtail T modifieds running Ford V8 engines at the lakes before World War II. It was a "run what ya brung" time and everyone had a ball.

Stu Hilborn's jet black B Class streamliner. Ran 134 mph the first time Stu had everything together in 1942. The car turned 139.96 in 1947 running a 1934 flathead V8. That's "gettin it on" without trick fuel!

Chuck Abbott's '29 roadster pickup, which he ran on the streets of Glendale in the late '30s. A genuine "ticket-grabber" for those days.

This unidentified "boat tail" roadster is unusual even for a lakes meet. Engine looks like a flathead V-12 of some sort.

one-half seconds. Radio Gardner was showing an Air Force general this fueling thing, and the guy says, "That's pretty good, but we fuel in the air," and Radio says, "How's 115 gals in nine an a half seconds grab ya?" The general didn't believe it. It was a nitrogen system. They outlawed them after a couple guys had fires. Rutman had a fire. Someone else too, so they figured it was too dangerous.

TOM: After all this hot rodding stuff, as you look back on it, was it worth all the action?

CHUCK: You make so many friends, true friends, all the money in the world wouldn't buy them. And that means more to me than anything. When you have a lot of friends, you're happy.

TOM: Howard Johansen is a legend within legends of hot rodding, what happened in your experiences with Howard?

CHUCK: I met Howard up at El Mirage right after World War II, he had a twin tank with a chain-driven engine in one side and the driver in the other side. I happened to be on the SCTA technical committee, and I saw that the drag link between the steering and the pitman arm was just butt welded, and it didn't look too good at that, so I turned him down on the inspection. Howard never said a word, he just said OK, and they just put it on a trailer, and off they went. Later on we talked about it, and laughed, and he said the inspection was right. Howard was another major contributor to hot rodding, a real innovator.

Typical '32 Ford lakes roadster awaits the starter's signal at a 1947 SCTA El Mirage lake meet.

TOM: As I remember he was one of the first guys to put a set of those Speedway wheels on a dyno to move it outside. He had those dyno duels with Tony Capana, put wheels on it so he could get it out where Tony could hear it.

CHUCK: He was running a GMC on the dyno one time and the mixture was a little lean. They burned a hole in the piston, so they just pulled the head, he welded up the hole in the piston, they put the head back on and that night they ran the engine at Carrol Speedway.

TOM: You were saying something about a driveshaft he welded up.

CHUCK: One night the driveshaft broke, so he went over to the fellow who had the welding truck, wanted to use the welder. The guy asked what he wanted to do, and he said he was gonna weld a driveshaft back together. The truck owner said it wouldn't hold, Howard said it would. The guy says, 'I'm

This car has been identified as the original Bob Rufi Chevy 4 modified that preceded his famous 143.161 mph aluminum projectile. Muroc Dry Lake in the soft helmet and goggle days.

Glendale Sidewinder Roadsters at the lakes. Right to left, Yam Oka's #236 roadster, Kong Jackson at the wheel of the R.H. roadster, Fred Huber the passenger.

Formerly the Bob Rufi streamliner that set the 1940 SCTA streamliner record of 140.00 mph. Looks like it used speedway tires on the rear.

a certified welder, and it won't hold." Howard said, "I'm a certified aircraft welder, and I'll take a chance." Well, five years later that car still had the welded driveshaft in it.

TOM: When the small blocks came out, I'd go down there and Howard was running them on the dyno. I'd ask him where he got them because no one else had them, and he said, "I got a whole bunch of them in that shed over there, whenever the guys ruin one, I get it and patch it up and work it."

CHUCK: Innovators like that just don't exist today, I don't think. Like the Bustle Bomb. Wasn't that the dragster that had a Cad in the front and an Olds in the rear? That was innovative. Howard went to Florida one time with a DeSoto in a boat, and he sank it. Everybody down there was real happy, because they figured they were gonna get beat anyway, they figured he couldn't get the boat running by the next day. He got it running that night, all cleaned up, and the next day he went out and won everything.

TOM: He was telling me one time of another thing that they did, where the engines were stuffed back in the cowl in the track roadsters. Where the back two cylinders were under the cowl, they were running the two cylinders at the back with big bores. When the inspectors would tech them, the team would pull the head off, and the inspectors would mike the bores they could get at easy. Never did check the back holes.

CHUCK: When he moved down to Paris he was dry farming, and he had a wheat combine down there. He'd gone through it and put servo motors in there, and hydraulic cylinders to do away with some of the chains and belts. He had that combine all powered, great piece of farm equipment.

TOM: I talked to him one time and asked if he'd been shooting any ducks. He was all banged up with arthritis. He said yes, as he'd built him a little thing he could sneak through the grass on. It was sort of like a motorized creeper. It was amazing to go to a surplus store with him. You'd go walking through there, and he could see parts all done in his mind. I saw stuff and wondered what it could be used for, he already had an idea and could see it in his mind.

CHUCK: He would never finish a lot of things, either. He'd do one thing and pretty soon he was off into boats, or dragsters, or stuff really weird. Boy, he had fun.

TOM: He used to tear them up at Bonneville, because they never knew what he was going to show up with. He had that Marmon…

Don Blair at the wheel of his famous "Goat" with blown Ford V8. This car originally belonged to the Spalding Brothers.

A trio of street roadsters in front of Evans Products, home of Evans Speed Equipment.

CHUCK: The cylinders in that Marmon were so tough he had a hard time boring the engine. It had sleeves in it, and they were so tough that the boring bar chattered in it. Guys used to hate to see him coming. Even at the track, whatever class he was running in. He ran roadsters, Andy Linden drove for him, and others. At first it was a four-port Riley, then he went into Jimmys. His cams were not the most accurate to lobe, but they sure ran like gangbusters. For sure nobody could copy them.

Like I say, there were some genuine innovators in early hot rodding, more so than today. Even so, this is a great sport. Frankly, I never considered I'd ever think of it as having a history.

Chuck Abbott on the starting line in his Model A-V8 roadster. This is the car he drove to Bonneville in 1947 to see John Cobb's streamliner and the Novi Indy car run on the salt.

STAN BETZ

TOM: Stan Betz is known in Southern California as one of the top paint mixers/matchers and what have you, but a lot of people don't realize that he has been a hot rodder for a long time. So, I'm going to start out by asking how did you get started with this whole thing, how old were you and all those good things?

STAN: When I was 10 years old I started working with my uncle, Dick Kraft, who was already running at the dry lakes before World War II. I would take the engine out, and he would work on the engine, then I would put it back in. So I got my start in mechanics when I was 10 years old. When I was 12 years old, I went out and bought a '29 roadster, and I paid $50 for it, that was down in San Pedro. We hauled it home on a rope, it wouldn't run. We had a large avocado tree in the backyard, we pulled the Model A motor out so then we bought a '32 engine that Jimmy Palm had in his roadster. It was a stock engine, he had just bought a '32 roadster and he put a '59 A block in his.

TOM: Did you use the '32 crossmembers?

STAN: Yeah, the '32 crossmembers, a typical A-V8. I got started with an early model engine, and I got some experience with my uncle when he was working on his and so duplicated as much as possible to my engine as he was working on his. Then when I was 14, I ran a little bit at the lakes.

TOM: Were you running El Mirage then?

STAN: No, we ran at Harper Lakes. Then after World War II, it got going real good, and we started running at El Mirage. I was in high school and I joined the Lancers Car Club, it met in Hollywood then.

Stan Betz with a chopped 1940 Deluxe convertible, his wheels while attending Anaheim High School in 1946.

Here is uncle Dick Kraft holding court in his drag racing creation, "The Bug"— Santa Ana Drag Strip, 1950. The days of real sport!

TOM: What was this about the streamliner you mentioned?

STAN: Oh, yeah. We had a narrow Essex frame in which we put this early model engine that was really putting out the horsepower, we had a sprint car tail and a cowl on it. The car weighed about 1,100 pounds and the hood was made out of a Coca-Cola sign. Actually, we had the record for eight months in this B Class streamliner class, it was open wheel at the time.

TOM: What was the record?

STAN: We went 136 mph. Then we started running the drags in 1950 out at Santa Ana Airport. My uncle started, he used just the frame and a little cowl and that was the start of what came to be called the dragster. He ran out there for about a year and a half. He was always in the top eliminator, and he would usually have to run off with Chet Herbert's motorcycle, "The Beast."

TOM: How about street racing and driving stuff, what was going on then?

STAN: We used to go to Picadilly Restaurant out in Sepulveda every Saturday night. There was a little small road out there that we used to drag race on. Some of the time we would lose an engine, and we would have to tow it back with a rope all the way to Orange County which was about 40 miles. Or tear out a transmission or tear out an axle, and we would have to tow it all the way back. As soon as we would see some lights coming fast we knew it was the cops so we would

Troy Ruttman in 1946 when he started his career driving roadsters on the oval tracks. Troy went on to be a top handler in the midgets and "Big Cars," winning the Indy 500 in 1952 in the Agajanian Special.

Dick Kraft's 92-inch wheelbase, 1,400-pound beauty was a real head turner" back in 1954 when it graced the cover of the October issue of HOT ROD MAGAZINE. Art Ingels, master aluminum man hand formed the .064-3-S half-hard aluminum body. The car was powered with a Ford V8-60 engine running Edelbrock heads and manifold along with a Potvin cam. Dick ran a Class C streamliner at the lakes in 1947. That's Stan on the left, Dick Kraft on the right.

How 'bout louvered moon discs? Stan Betz was doing just that for customers, and Dean Moon himself, at his shop back in 1957. Artwork on shop truck is by Von Dutch.

Southern California's master custom auto paint mixer, Stan Betz, and the master of the striping brush, Von Dutch, eyeball a restored motorcycle that Von Dutch has just finished.

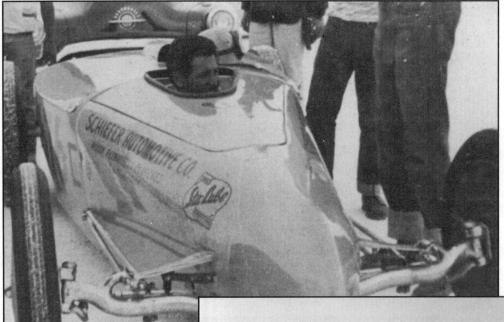

Paul Schiefer in his beautiful rear engine T Bonneville roadster. Every car Paul ran at the salt or lakes was of outstanding quality.

Sandy Belond's '32 roadster waits in line during a pre-war lakes meet. How 'bout those inside, outside white walls.

all head in a different direction.

TOM: There were a lot of good places to run then.

STAN: Orange County was close to Los Alamitos Naval Station where they had the ammo dump. There was a road in between the ammo dump that was really isolated from anything else, and we used to race out there on Friday nights. People would bet against each other and a certain person would hold all the money, it became quite a gambling sport out there at that ammo dump. Five dollars in those days was good money. That was our weekly mad money that we would gamble with. Then the drags got to be quite a big thing, and people would come from all over. At first it was only the Orange County participants, then Los Angeles. I was working as a mechanic down in Balboa at an amusement place, it was called the Bay Arcade which was owned by a senator from Texas.

Howard Hughes and Lana Turner used to come through there and we used to talk with them, and then Humphrey Bogart would come stumbling through there when he would come from the bar. He wouldn't stay long, he would be pretty looped up. He had to try to find his boat. Johnny Wisemueller was always walking through there when he was training down there for the Olympics. I also saw Tommy Dorsey, and there was Glen Miller, the Modernaires, and Stan Kenton. Saturday night you would be lucky to find a place to park. Then on Easter week, all the hot rods from Southern California would gather and also the custom cars and we would go out on Pacific Coast Highway and have a few races. There were a lot of cars that Barris would work on that would show up at Balboa.

TOM: Were you doing any paint work then at all?

STAN: No, I started with a louver machine. Frank Kurtis' foreman had a louver machine, and he told me what kind of tube steel to get to make the die and he showed me how to make the clearance so the metal wouldn't rip. In about three weeks, I had the louver machine going. That was a big fad for about four years before it started to die down. A friend of mine used to work out at Rinshed Mason in the paint lab, and he said, "Why don't you sell a little paint as well, because the louvers aren't keeping you busy." So for $800 I got the franchise for the R&M Paint Co. Actually we would mix the bright colors for the hot rods when they would have the hoods louvered and then the used car lots saw the colors we were mixing, so they started painting their used cars with bright colors because it became a fad.

We started to really get going with all of the used car lots, and then we got slowly started with the body shops. We would have to go out to the factory and pick up the the paint because it would have to be a factory packaged paint. Since we started with such little funding, we would have to go out to the factory and pick up a six pack of quarts of a certain color, and if the body shop wanted two quarts then we would put four quarts on the shelf. That's how we started with $800 in the paint business. But, it started to branch out a little more and then before we knew it

Manuel Ayulo, one of the early CRA pioneers, in his '32 Street roadster converted to circle track use, 1946. For more on track roadsters, see Tex Smith's book, Roaring Roadsters.

Jack McGrath, another of the dry lakes runners who switched over to oval track racing, went on to be an Indy 500 star along with his pal Manny Ayulo, both were from the Southern California area.

The full belly panned '25 T roadster entered by Stanley Betz. qualified at over 120 mph with its 170-inch Ford V8-60 engine. Bonneville Nationals, 1953.

The full belly-panned '25 T roadster entered by Stanley Betz qualified at over 120 mph with its 170-inch Ford V8-60 engine. Bonneville Nationals, 1953.

we were the top paint store in Orange County out of 32 stores, and we won a trip to Las Vegas. After that we got in with the aircraft companies and we did special work for them, the last job we did was the interior colors for the Space Lab. Also, we've done quite a few colors for movie stars.

TOM: Where you doing the stuff for Gil Ayala and Barris and those guys?

STAN: Yeah, in fact we still do work for Barris. Gil would always come down on Saturday and we would mix his colors for him.

TOM: When did you first get interested in or go to Bonneville?

STAN: Oh, we went to Bonneville in '57 and ran A Class Roadster. That was a '54 engine, 180 cubic inches. We went 126 mph. Ray Brown ran an A Class Roadster also, but we would usually have to take second place to him because he ran pretty good. He had access to a wind tunnel and all that stuff. We were kind of small boys.

TOM: How long have you been down there where you are now, down by the Big A stadium in Anaheim?

STAN: I've been there 19 years.

TOM: Tell me about flying the streamliner.

STAN: At the lakes when we were running the streamliner, it was with a small engine. Just before they were going to shut down, the wind was coming up. I guess I was the last car through, and

The Chrisman Brothers and Duncan from Compton, California, entered this slippery competition coupe in both B and C Classes. Turned 163.63 mph with a Merc engine in C Class and was the 1953 Bonneville Nats B competition coupe and sedan record holder with a two-way average speed of 160.78 mph running a 258 Merc engine.

OFFICIAL PROGRAM
GILMORE GOLD CUP ROAD RACE

Program cover of the Gilmore Gold Cup Road Race, held on the "B" shaped course at Mines Field, Inglewood, California, February 18, 1934. Event was sponsored by the Gilmore Oil Company and promoted by Bill Pickens. Of the 28 cars entered, nearly all were '34 Ford roadsters minus fenders, but stock in the engine department. Rex Mays started on the pole, winner was Stubby Stubblefield, Al Gordon second. Total elapsed time for the 250 mile race was 4 hours, 14 seconds.

A Southern Speedway race program cover for August 2, 1936. Southern Speedway was located at Atlantic and Tweedy Blvd. in Southgate, a suburb of L.A. Home of the modified roadster races, this track was a training ground for many later to be famous race drivers. This 1936 program listed about every four-cylinder conversion for Ford engines known to man. One Ford V8-powered car was listed in the program.

the car got caught in the wind. It went 17 feet up in the air. It come down on all four. It was a long ways up there.

TOM: You've been restoring and building a few things?

STAN: Well, I have a 1934 Indianapolis car that Pop Dreyer built when he had a shop on 16th Street in Indianapolis. The car had a flathead at Indianapolis and it didn't do much against the Miller cars. Then I have a 1940 Ford convertible sedan that I showed at the Oakland Roadster Show, which was built on a Corvette chassis. I bought a roll-over Corvette, and we used the complete chassis and the motor, transmission, rear end and front suspension. We had to cut the cowl and the deck lid and widen the car out because the Corvette wheel tread is so wide. We had to add seven inches to the body. Then we had to cut the hood in the center and put a pie-shaped piece in the hood. We had seven inches in the cowl and at the front of the hood we only had two inches so it wouldn't get out of proportion. Then we

As can be seen by these post-war race program covers, the hot rod roadsters were off and running on circle tracks in all parts of California.

had to put a little space between the '40 grille, a little wider chrome strip in the center, and also we had to add 2 1/2 inches to the fenders so it would fit. It come out pretty well proportioned.

The Betz-Louver City Special still on the trailer prior to qualifying in the A Modified Roadster Class with a speed of 120.48 mph at the Bonneville Nationals, 1953.

Unidentified Bonneville tank sponsored by Grant Piston Rings gets ready for a blast down the salt. A very clean looking racer.

Stan Betz with one of the unusual cars that have come under his gifted hand. His enthusiasm for hot rodding is as strong today as it was in the '30s.

TOM: You had a '36 or a '40 before, when you were a young lad?

STAN: Yeah, when I was a kid. That was a tow car. The last car we had at Oakland was a '47 Woody that we built out of a '85 Corvette. We used the Corvette doors and the windshield, then we fabricated the quarter panels and we lengthened the car a foot. Then we put a steel top in and the top does lift off. We got first place in our class at Oakland, with both cars. Then we went to Blacky Gegian's show in Fresno and got first place in that too.

TOM: What are you going to do now on the new paints, is all that stuff phasing in?

STAN: Eventually, we will be using water base paints, with lights to dry it out.

TOM: Is it like a two process thing, where you put the flat coat on, then the clear?

STAN: Yeah, you use the same urethane clear as we use today, but over the water base. That way by using the water base under base and the clear over the top it

The So-Cal Speed Shop Special, Bonneville, 1949. This Xydias and Batchelor streamliner captured the A Class Streamliner record at the 1st Bonneville Nats with a two-way average of 156.39 mph. This sleek beauty also ran 187.89 mph topping the C Class Streamliner at the same event.

passes the emissions standards that the state of California demands.

TOM: How is that stuff for repairing and matching?

STAN: You have to have ultraviolet lights even for repair because the water base dries so slowly that you have to speed up the process so you can get your car out where you can put the clear on.

The SCTA timing crew at the lights during the first Bonneville Nats in 1949. The theme of the first Bonneville was "Run And Have Fun!"

An early Ford V-8 powered T modified owned and driven by George Yamase. Note the "sling shot" dual carburetor manifold.

Spalding Brothers' pre-war modified. Ford V8 was fitted with a set of Riley OHV heads, Mercedes blower and a pair of Stromberg carbs. Ran 138 mph.

DON FRANCISCO

I first met Don Francisco when he came to work for *HOT ROD MAGAZINE* as a tech editor in the early '50s. I was already there, shooting pictures, drawing cartoons and things. I knew Don from the lakes and his involvement with Bill Burke and their 150 mph belly tank, but I got to know him very well at the magazine. Don and I worked together at HRM for a number of years. We also worked on *MOTOR TREND* together. We would go on road tests, or out to Indio to do braking tests. Sometimes the methods were crude, but it was always fun.

Prior to joining the HRM staff, Don worked for the fire department in Monterey Park. He also had a shop there, and I would drive over to see him in my A-V8 coupe. All the guys would hang around because they all wanted to make their cars go a little quicker, and Don's shop was where it would happen. The shop is where I met Ray Brock.

Don built lots of engines, including a flathead for my '41 Ford that I drove to Indianapolis the first year I covered the race. I drove all the way back, raced everybody in sight, and never had any trouble coming

or going. I always laugh about that trip, the company paid for the gas.

Later on I had a '49 Ford convertible that I bought from my boss, Bob Petersen. I ran it for a year or so, but everybody was getting overhead valve happy, so Don suggested we put an Olds and a Hydramatic in it. We ended up making the swap at his shop at night. Every day after work I'd jump in my Model A coupe and race over to Monterey Park, and we'd work 'til 2:30 or 3:00 in the morning, race home, then get up and go to work. We had a great time together working on that, and countless other projects.

Don and I went back to Indy several times, we stayed in a rooming house right across from the Speedway. We'd spend all day at the track.

One thing I'll always remember about Don; whenever he was working on something, I'd do all the grunt work. I'd take something apart and take it over to him an ask if we were going to use it and his famous words were, "wash it up and we'll take a look at it." Uncle Donald is one of the nicest guys I know, and we've been friends for a long time.

This photo of the starting line could be any lakes meet, any year, only the passenger cars and pickups are a giveaway to the year.

TOM: Remember the first time you went to the lakes?

DON: I got out of high school in '35 and started buying motorcycles. My first trip to the lakes was on a '36 Indian Chief. That first trip I went to Muroc, and that was my first exposure to the lakes.

TOM: You must have seen Rufi's streamliner run.

DON: Oh, yes. That was quite a car.

TOM: Did you know the Spalding boys, Tom and Bill?

DON: I met them later, after I got on the *HOT ROD MAGAZINE* staff. I didn't meet many guys in those early years. We'd just go out to the lakes and watch 'em run and have fun.

TOM: How'd you get hooked up with Bill Burke?

DON: When I first saw Burke he was still wearing his sailor suit, he'd built this belly tank with a torch and old coat hangers for welding rod. I don't know how much he'd run it before I got involved, but the gist of it was, he had a car but with nothing to make it go, and I was building engines.

TOM: You were working with the fire department then?

DON: Yeah, the Alhambra fire department. Burke and I formed a partnership then.

TOM: This had to be when, '46?

The Babler-Ulrich 1932 Ford three-window coupe ran in D Class, turned 127 mph.

DON: Yeah, '45-'46, somewhere in there. I worked for the fire department from '42 to '49, then I went to work for the magazine. So it was in the later part of the '40s when we formed a partnership on the car. He would take care of the car, the chassis and

The big change in 1960 dry lakes racing came with modern engines to replace the venerable Ford flathead V8, this very large GMC supercharger on a small block Chevy ohv is a prime example.

Corvette entered by Automotive Specialty ran 141.509 mph against a record of 150, earning points for the Rod Riders club.

stuff like that, and I would take care of the engine and transmission, and together we'd take care of the driveline.

TOM: You must have done a pretty good face lift on the thing.

DON: Not a whole lot, actually. You know the entire time we ran we had one engine. We'd put it together and run it, change the oil every once in a while. We'd buy a set of pistons for eight dollars, cams and heads were available. We were running triple Strombergs with straight alcohol, and we just ran and had a lot of fun. We were the first to run a water tank instead of a radiator, a big tank behind the driver. We'd run it, bring it back, change the water, run it again. It worked great, in fact I saw a couple at Bonneville this last trip, they were running the same sorta thing. We had about 40 gallons of water.

TOM: That was good for the weight too. Was that a rear-engine tank?

DON: It was rear engined, the driver sat up front. We didn't have a quick change, so we got somebody to build one. It was based on an A rearend and they built a set of straight cut gears, three to one; it sounded like a siren, but it worked. We ran street tires, no such thing as speed-rated tires in those days. Later we got involved in some old Indy tires. Anyway, we ran a few years, like that and had a lot of fun.

TOM: You guys were the first to go 150 mph, right?

DON: I think so, but I think at the same meet we did that, Stu Hillborn with his streamliner with a flathead in it beat us by about one mile an hour. He was just starting to work on his fuel injector then. We ran at Bonneville, went up there in '49, and I think our fastest speed there was 164.

Highboy roadsters have been a mainstay of hot rodding seemingly forever, but the tall cars are tough to make go fast.

Tom: Billy Fry drove it, didn't he?

Don: He drove, Wally Parks drove, and then there was another guy, I can't remember his name, but any ways, that guy, we'll call him number two, we were at El Mirage one time, he'd made a run and was coming back when a big dust storm came up and he drove right into a line of guys who were waiting to go. He crashed our car, and a couple others. Nothing serious, no one got hurt, just bent up a little metal, that's the thing I remember him for. Billy Fry may hold the record at Bonneville for being the first to go through the traps backwards. He spun just before getting to the traps and went through backwards at about 150.

Tom: Remember in Monterey Park, I had my A coupe, Ray Brock was coming around, and you guys were putting a Chrysler in your Ford coupe?

Don: Brock lived just a few blocks from the shop and he kept wandering in. We got aquatinted and he helped me on a few things.

Tom: When we were putting the Olds in my '49 Ford, he built my headers. I called 'em Brock flow headers because they had so many leaks in them.

Don: I had a Ford business coupe that I bought new in 1950. It was 800 and some dollars. After about two years the engine started getting tired, so I bought a new Chrysler Hemi for 800 bucks. I made up an adapter plate and put the Hemi against the stock transmission. It didn't need low gear, just put it in second, and if you mashed on it too hard the transmission fell out. That happened three times. Then I went and bought a

This supercharged flathead engine with carburetors is timeless.

brand new Hydramatic and that was still in it when I sold the car to my nephew years and years later.

Tom: You came over to work at *HOT ROD MAGAZINE* when I was there. Wally must have recruited you.

Front mounted superchargers, as on this Chrysler Hemi, were a common sight at lakes and drags well into the '60s.

"come to work for me." So I was making $305 a month at the fire department and Bob Lindsey, one of the bosses, said they'd pay me more than that. So *HOT ROD* paid me $308 to start, but there was a chance for advancement. I was tired of the fire department anyway, and I'm not really a team player. Besides I had managed to get a captain unhappy with me, and he was loading all the crap on me, which I didn't like, so I was kinda eager to get out of there. So

DON: Yeah, that's when I was working at the fire department. I knew Wally from the lakes. Wally told me one time that he needed an article on ignition systems, and I said, "good luck." So he said, "I want you to do it," and I said I didn't know anything about writing. He said to just try it. I had spare time, so I wrote it and sent it in and he printed it. Then I did another article or two that way, and then he said, anyway, I worked for Wally and Pete, and Bob while he was there, until I quit in 1953.

TOM: After you left the magazine you went to work on the Mexican road race with the Lincolns didn't you?

DON: I worked for Bill Stroppe and Clay Smith on the cars, preparing them, then took them down on trucks. The first year I worked as one of the crew members on Chuck Daigh and Chuck Stevenson's car. Every night we'd take 'em apart, fix 'em, and put 'em back together. The following year I went down as a crew chief.

TOM: After every leg of the race could you work on the cars as long as you wanted or was there a time limit?

DON: I don't remember if there was a time limit, but we had plenty of time. Mostly it was brake work, wheels and tires, once in a while we had to replace a transmission. Vern Houle was the transmission man. He could change one of them in about 20 minutes, it could be

red hot, with steaming oil runnin' all over, and he'd get it done. He later rode with Vukovich.

TOM: You also went to the East African Safari didn't you?

DON: Yes, I was on that one year.

TOM: When did you guys start the Baja thing?

DON: That was in 1967, the Mexican 1,000. I wasn't really involved in that first thing. Ed Perlman was putting it on and he didn't have any way to get around down there, so I flew him around in my airplane. The next year I bought the other guy out, Pete Condos, so then we put them on till '73 or so.

MICKEY THOMPSON'S CHALLENGER I

Back in 1959, Don Francisco wrote an article for *ROD BUILDER* magazine concerning land speed record attempts by Mickey Thompson.

Sixteen out of a possible 18 figures almost 89 percent for most people, but for Mickey Thompson it comes out an even zero. Although Mickey drove his Challenger I to 16 new land speed records October 6 on the Bonneville Salt Flats, he isn't too impressed because he missed the big one of 394 mph held since 1947 by the late John Cobb of England.

Distances and speeds for Mickey's records are:

5 kilometers	345.33 mph
5 miles	340.70 mph
10 kilometers	327.59 mph
10 miles	286.16 mph

These are all "flying" records, which means the car had a running start, and all records are subject to FIA confirmation.

Although there are only four distances and speeds involved, they amount to 16 records because each of them goes in four different record books: World's Unlimited, International Class A, National Class Unlimited (US), and National Class A (US).

Mickey feels certain he would have captured the big one if conditions on the salt had been better. His runs were delayed two weeks by an unseasonable rainstorm. Threats of more rain forced him to make his runs before the salt was as dry as it should have been. The course was also shorter than desired. The slippery salt made acceleration very difficult, while at speed there was enough tire slippage to keep the car in the 360 mph area.

As an anticlimax Mickey came close to losing the car and himself on a run he made later in the afternoon of his records. He was testing fuel and gearing changes when at some point on a run his oxygen mask hose disconnected from the tank. He lost consciousness. The last thing he remembers about the run is that a little voice told him to pop the chute. When crew members lifted the cockpit cover, Mickey's chin was on his chest. They reconnected the oxygen tube and he soon regained consciousness.

Mickey Thompson was an extremely innovative hot rodder at both the drag strip and at Bonneville, this car was the first serious challenge to John Cobb's land speed record.

Thompson's streamliner ran four Pontiac engines, which wasn't particularly unusual for the time, but it was perhaps one of the most successful.

lasted. We also had the races at Parker, we called it the Dam 500 and the Parker 500. My partner, Perlman got the idea.

TOM: Your place in Pasadena, that's a place for off-road stuff?

DON: Yeah there were two of them actually. One of them I started in 1973 or so with Sandy Cohen. We made front end bars and roll bars for Jeep Cherokees. We sold wheels and tires, but Sandy got an offer of a job where he could make more money, and then the guy we were renting from wanted his

We had the Baja 500 and the Mexican 1,000 that went all the way to La Paz. The 500 started and ended in Ensenada. The races aren't the same now because they're paving everything down there. It was a one-track dirt thing then, it was a lot of fun while it

building back, or more rent or something. Perlman wasn't doing anything, I got him interested, we found a building on Colorado Boulevard, and he an I started the Baja 500 Off Road Store. No manufacturing, we sold wheels and tires.

Coupes and sedans were not allowed in some of the early SCTA events, one reason for other types of associations, such as Russetta.

THE WRITING OF DON FRANCISCO

For several years in the mid-1950s, Don Francisco was Technical Editor at HOT ROD MAGAZINE. After that, he continued to contribute articles on a wide variety of subjects. Whereas many writers would have a problem in filling a magazine page, Cisco would invariably provide far too much, causing no end of consternation to Bob Greene, the Managing Editor/Editor. In searching out information on Don Francisco, we ran across some notes and photos he *collected back in 1960 for a story on his return to the dry lakes. Rather than rely on his scrapbook, we thought it would be fun to include this material as a kind of bridge between hot rodding before the '60s, and what would come later. Unlike what we did in those early HRM days, I've left the text unedited so that what you read is pure Don Francisco.*

—Tex Smith

OUTLINE FOR *HOT ROD MAGAZINE* STORY, by Don Francisco

Legal competitive hot rodding, as a non-professional sport, originated on dry lakes of Southern California. This was years before anyone thought of legalized drag racing. Muroc dry lake, ideal for high speed straightway events (except for the ever-present dust) was the center of this top-speed activity until it was taken

over by the U.S. Government as a military aircraft test center. This is now Edward's Air Force Base.

Ousted from Muroc, hot rodders wandered back and forth between Rosamond, Evans, and El Mirage, and finally settled at El Mirage. None of those dry lakes were anything like Muroc, either in size or surface, but El Mirage was the best of what was available.

For a few days after WW II, I was a constant competitor at the lakes. Then, for one reason or another, I drifted away. This visit for the Russetta Timing Association event on July 19, 1960 was my first time back in eight or nine years.

It brought back memories of things I hope I shall never forget.

Time hasn't changed El Mirage. It is the same sun dried flat spot in the middle of a high desert, with the same dust and the same afternoon wind. At first glance, the cars appeared the same as I remembered, with the exception of the late model

stockers. There were A roadsters, belly tanks, Deuce roadsters, coupes of all years, sprint type track jobs... nothing much different from what I knew nearly a decade ago.

Until the hoods were opened.

In most of them, the flathead Ford V8s or six cylinder Chevy/ GMC engines

have been superseded by overhead valve V8s. Small block Chevys and big Hemi Chryslers predominate, with an assorted lot of Dodge, Cad, and Olds. Superchargers are on some. These modern powerplants have had an understandable influence on the vehicle speeds. When Bill Burke and I retired our flathead Merc-powered belly tank from competition, it held the class record

with a speed of 164 mph. At this meet, a '29 A roadster with a blown Chevy turned 189.075 mph, which was the day's fastest. Another roadster with a flathead turned 174. In all fairness, the flathead performance must be considered the exception rather than the rule.

In all, there were 48 cars at this meet, entered in 22 classes.

DUFFY LIVINGSTONE

TOM: So, you were in the Navy, right?

DUFFY: Yeah, four years.

TOM: You mentioned PUI's and stuff?

DUFFY: Yeah, I went in March '42 and went to boot camp in San Diego, then they shipped me off to Jacksonville, Florida, for aviation machinist mate training. Then we went up to Norfolk, Virginia, to a kind of a holding tank. It was a building they used for a grinder in the winter time. Anyway, they had bunks in there, it was just a holding tank at the time, no grinder, for guys to be relocated in different places. One day there was a shipment of 700 guys who left the building, and you couldn't tell they were gone. Then I hopped on a ship and went out to sea and headed for Greenland. A friend of mine that I grew up and went to school with, joined the Navy a year or two before I did. I had lost track of him. We were on a ship going down to Panama, when we were about two days out I was walking down a passageway and here comes a guy out of the engine room. I ran right into him and it was Bob Greenaway, my childhood buddy.

TOM: Now, when did you get out of the service?

Duff himself at El Mirage in the late '40s with his flathead Caddy V8-powered '32 roadster. The car ran 113 mph.

A three-quarter view of Duffy's '32. The rags sticking out of the side panel are plugging up the exhaust stacks of the flathead Caddy V8.

DUFFY: I got out in 1946.

TOM: What did you do then? How did you get into the muffler and welding business?

DUFFY: After I was discharged I got on the 52-20 and just messed around and somehow, I'm not sure how, found that Dave Mitchell had a roadster for sale. He was down in Las Tunis, and I went down and he had a '32 roadster for sale, so I bought it. I got acquainted with Mitch and he talked me into putting a Cadillac engine into it. So, I put in a flathead Cad and '39 LaSalle transmission.

TOM: Yeah, those were the good ones. What kind of manifold was on that thing? I noticed you were running two Strombergs.

DUFFY: Well, it had a stock manifold that we made into a dual. We cut the manifold in half and put a piece of water hose between the two halves for balance. It had two of the big Stromberg carburetors on it. In fact, I loaned that manifold to George Dunah and he went up to Bonneville with it and ran 150 mph with his old '29.

TOM: How fast did your car run?

DUFFY: I think it was about 113 mph or something like that. I ran it with SCTA and

This overhead view shows Duffy Livingstone's '32 roadster with trick outside headers installed. A very neat looking setup.

Duff's Deuce roadster showing the accepted front suspension set-up of the time. Juice brakes, "Dago" front axle, tube shocks and dropped headlight bar.

Here's Duffy's '32 roadster in street attire. Check out the smooth looking '41 Ford dash layout.

Russetta a few times. I'd take the lights and the windshield off and go out and race. Anyway, I still have some old SCTA timing tags around here, in fact I put one on my '27 that I have now and the kids around here don't know what the hell is going on. That tag was on a '32 channeled roadster with a Merc in it that ran 113. So anyway, I put this tag on my dashboard and the ET (Elapsed Time) was 7.90, or something like that. The kids look at it and ask how I turned a 7.90 and only went 113!

TOM: When did you go to work for Mitchell Muffler?

DUFFY: We got to be pretty good buddies

Here's a look at the mighty Caddy flathead V8. The intake manifold was homemade, and ran two 97s. The exhaust manifold had two configurations; the one pictured is for street use, running pipes inside the frame. The upper three capped openings are for outside lakes headers.

and then he moved up to east Pasadena, up by the Rose Bowl, and he had Mitchell's Welding. I went to work for him there, I learned how to weld from ol' Mitchell.

TOM: I didn't meet you until I used to hang around Blair's. You guys were down there on Colorado and

Hudson, weren't ya?

DUFFY: Yeah, when he was out in east Pasadena, he went from Mitchell's Welding to Mitchell's Muffler. He started doing muffler work and handling Porter Mufflers, and then he moved into Pasadena over on Hudson and Colorado. He says he had asked everyone that produced steel-packed mufflers and none of them would run steel packs on their own cars because they are too loud. So he decided he would come up with something different.

I think the English already had glass-packed mufflers, they had them in their Jags and MGs. So anyway, Mitch says, "Let's make one and pack it with fiberglass." So I made the first glass-packed muffler for him and we packed it with this fiberglass like insulation. It sounded beautiful for about a week, and then the resin melted and the glass came seeping out. The guys driving behind ya would wonder why they were itching so much. Then Mitch came up with the idea of using roving, which is the remnants left on a spool of fiberglass, like string. So we used it and that seemed to hold up alright. That was the beginning of Mitchell Mufflers.

Earl Evans C Class belly tank lakester ran 185.86 mph at Bonneville in the early '50s. Powered by a 3/8 x 3/8 '46 Merc engine, using Evans heads and manifold with a Smith & Jones cam, #17 was the world's fastest unblown open wheeled car at that time. Earl's tank ran 181.08 mph at El Mirage, SCTA meet.

Duff's channeled '32 roadster, with Ford V8 power in street trim, ran 113 mph on El Mirage Dry Lake bed.

This tiny hand-built belly tank, owned by Fred Lobello of San Diego, was powered by a four-cylinder Ford engine equipped with a Riley four-port head. With only 214 cubic inches, this San Diego Roadster Club entry turned 139.75 mph at the '51 SCTA Bonneville meet.

TOM: So, he was probably one of the first to start making glass packs?

DUFFY: Yeah he was, started in about '48.

TOM: How did you get in the muffler business?

DUFFY: Roy Desbrow asked me if I'd like to go into a muffler business with him and I said, "why not." We got the back half of the old Colorado shop and put a hoist in there. In fact, we didn't have a hoist right at the start, I remember the first job we did was $66 on the creepers. I don't remember what happened, but we moved out to Monrovia and started our own muffler shop. We started manufacturing our own glass-pack mufflers, and we took on a third partner, Bud Morrill. We had a manufacturing company up in Altadena and then we figured that we ought to consolidate. So that's why we moved out to Monrovia into an old gas station. Like a bunch of dummies, we took the old glass gravity flow pumps and threw them away.

We built a building out back to manufacture the mufflers in, it was about 40' x 20'. Over the period of a couple years, I doubled the size of the building. All the structure was made out of muffler tubing. When we moved in, we asked the guys at City Hall what we should do with the gas tanks, and they said, "Oh, just fill them full of water and soluble oil, and it will be OK." So we did that and after many many years some new fireman came around inspecting the place. He asked what we had in the tanks, and I told him water and soluble oil. He told us that we had to get rid of that, either take the tanks out or fill them full of sand. I said, "Nope, not going to do that." The fireman said, "Sorry it's the law, you'll have to."

And I said, "Sorry, I'll move first. We checked with City Hall, and this is what they told us to do. Tell whoever you got to tell, that I'm not going to do it."

A few days later, the fire chief came down and said, "What in the hell are you doing to my new man?"

I said, "Well, we've been here for 20 years and everything has been cool and then this guy comes around and tells me I have to take these tanks out. The place isn't worth all that expense, I'm going to

The Pierson brothers' modified coupe ran 142.98 mph at a 1950 El Mirage Russetta meet. The car was powered by a full Edelbrock Ford V8 engine. It was a trend setter for the modified coupe class.

A typical '32 highboy lakes roadster from Santa Barbara, California. The tonneau cockpit cover helped reduce drag while making a speed run on the dry lake beds. Owner unknown.

move first."

The fire chief said, "Just go on down to City Hall and pay $3 for a permit to keep oil on your property and everything will be OK."

We stayed for a while longer, but muffler manufacturing was either get real big or just forget it, so we forgot it. So, we started two new muffler shops, Arubidoux Muffler out in Riverside, and Escondido Muffler, which I hear is now Advanced Muffler and is still running. Anyway, we sold those two and Roy and I were in Monrovia. I always was interested in cars, even as a kid I used to build model airplanes and model cars, and I think that old Gordon Babb, who owned Ace Model Shop back before the war, was the first person ever to put a model airplane engine in a car and on a tether. In fact I have a picture here somewhere. *POPULAR SCIENCE* magazine came out, they used to do little short subjects, they took us out to the Rose Bowl and they did a story on the thing. I've got a picture of me sitting there, it looks like I'm gutting a chicken, I got my hands down in the cockpit of this midget.

TOM: How did the go-kart thing come about?

DUFFY: Well, I knew Art Engles. I didn't know Lou Borelli that well, by the way he died just recently. I was into sporty car races, I bought a MG when I was with Mitchell, when he was down on Hudson in '52. That was about the time Roy and I went into the muffler business and we made a dual set for MGs. I remember I was down at Torrey Pines one day at a sporty car race, and we had some little cards printed up advertising a dual set for an MG. I remember there was a race going on, and here's this idiot sitting up on a top of a hill dusting his little MG off. I remember he had a leather cap and his girlfriend was sitting in the car. I went over and handed him a little card and he gave it back to me and said, "I don't want it to sound like no damn Chevy." Shortly after I started racing the old Eliminator T roadster.

TOM: How did that thing start about? Was it just something you wanted to build?

DUFFY: Well, I got interested in the sporty cars with the little MG, and it kind of looked like it would be fun. Do you remember Paul Parker?

This sharp looking B Class roadster, owned by Harvey Haller, was the top point getter for the Roadrunners Club during the '47 season. His V8-powered roadster ran Evans heads and manifold, turned a strong 128.57 mph at 1948 SCTA meet.

Bob Rounthwaite's chopped and channeled '34 three-window competition coupe turned 146.80 mph at El Mirage, and 154.905 at Bonneville in '51. Power was supplied by a 304-inch modified Merc V8 with Weiand four-carb manifold and heads. The cam was by Howard with a Harman-Collins 8R-101 mag making the fire. This car was featured in color in the October 1951 HOT ROD MAGAZINE.

TOM: Sure.

DUFFY: He had a Merc engine and I approached him, "You supply the engine and stuff, and I'll do the work on it. I've got a muffler shop, and we'll build the '25 T that we got from Jay Chamberlain. We'll build a hot rod and race it with the sporty cars."

Paul agreed so that's what we did. Paul Parker and I were in cahoots with each other, and we started building that on Hudson and Colorado before I went out to Monrovia. Funny thing is that I built some brackets that held the headlights and the old

Houdaille shocks. They were built in such a way that the shock went right to the top of the king pin on each side. Right out where it should be, ya know, and it was a headlight and a shock absorber bracket. I had a dual brake system, two master cylinders, this is back in '52-'53. The old hot rod used the model T spring that would clear the Halibrand center section. I built a plate in the back of the frame where you could adjust the height of the thing and the radius rods were like on midget, the two bars coming back into a single.

Bill Burke, long-time lakes and Bonneville participant, was the official starter for this El Mirage early '50s lakes meet. The Pierson brother's coupe is next up to run.

The Miller Crankshaft Special track roadster. Many of the track cars also ran the lakes in the late '40s. Rosie Roussel was the car's roundy round driver.

TOM: Yeah, the hairpin job.

DUFFY: *HOT ROD MAGAZINE* got a hold of all of it and came out and shot some pictures, I don't know if it was Rick or you, somebody did. They ran all four things in one of their little yearly how-to books, the radius rods, the adjustable rear end, the dual master cylinder, and the head light bracket, which was the only thing that worked. I could never get the two master cylinders synchronized good enough so that the car would stop right. The rear end, I got rid of that crap, threw the T spring away and put a '41 Ford rear end in it with the spring back enough to clear the center section of the Halibrand. That is the only

The crew of this flathead-powered T modified relaxes as they ponder a carburetor problem. You can bet they would be ready to run by the time they arrived at the starting line.

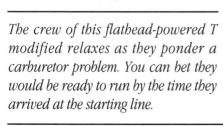

reason I put that spring back there, it was 17 feet behind the axle. and that is one of the best things I ever did to that car handling wise. The darn thing just came to life, just moving that spring back.

TOM: What was the wheelbase on that thing? It had to be pretty short.

DUFFY: I think it was 92 or 95 inches. It was so

Hollis "Haul-ee" Hedrich, hero handler, waits with his crew for the starter's signal at an early '50s lakes meet. Note the recycled hood panels.

short coupled it would run out at 120-125 mph and it would start to get a little side shuffle. Being almost square it wasn't stable enough on the top end, but it would corner like mad. After I got all my stuff together and got it sorted out, I never had any car challenge me or pass me in a corner.

TOM: What did everyone think the first time you took it out?

DUFFY: Aw, they laughed at me, it was painted pink with a Merc in it. It looked awful. Then, later, we got it cleaned up and then a little bit more. We raced the thing for nine years.

TOM: What were some of the funny incidents you can remember?

DUFFY: Well, ya know, even I could see that the more rubber you got on the ground the better that thing stuck. It weighed 2,150 with me in it and a half tank of fuel. I got a hold of a set of Goodyear Blue

A typical rear-engine belly tank lakester. This configuration was very popular right after the war as the surplus aircraft drop tanks were easy to obtain. Owner unknown.

Streaks that were made for the police department, and they had a lot of rubber for that era. The sporty car guys were running their little Pirelli bicycle tires, and I went down to this guy Cliff at Voigt tires in El Monte. I was running 6:50-16 slicks on the back, they were grooved and they were just not running smooth. So I bought a pair of Halibrand sprint car wheels, wide base jobs at the time, go-cart wheels are now that wide. Anyway, I went to Cliff and asked him to make the widest drag slick he had, told him what I wanted them for and asked him to groove 'em. They were half crude and half gum rubber, I put them on the car and in those days it looked like a steamroller. I rolled it into the tech inspectors and they said, "You can't run these tires."

I said, "Why can't I, the only thing it says in the book is that the tires have to have tread. All my other tires have this tread."

The inspectors said, "No, no, you just can't run these, they aren't sports car tires."

I said, "Well, what's a sports car tire?"

"Well, it's a tire on a sports car," they replied.

I said, "Well, how long have I been running this sucker as a sports car."

"Well, three years."

"Well, OK it's a sports car and the tires are on it, does that make them sport car tires?"

"No, you have to run Formula Libra."

At the time, they had a dozen Formula cars that Fangio and Phil Hill and all those guys drove from Europe. So I stripped the fenders, took the headlights off and left the horn connected and we had to start behind the consolation cars. I got to the point where I could blow off all the Formula

Bonneville is not all fun and games, as this photo shows. Bill Burke and crew are doing some serious wrenching on Bill's Ardun-Merc powered home-built fiberglass sports car. It paid off, he was first in his class at the 1953 Bonneville Nationals with a speed of 167 mph.

cars. then I thought I was going to be big time, so I put torsion bars on the the car and took it out to Pomona and man I couldn't get around a corner. I didn't know what I was doing, I still don't. Half of the

Wild looking T roadster. Check out the three-bump hood, must have some exotic engine beneath that great body work. Couldn't find anyone who could identify the car.

around a corner, but we pulled the flathead and stuck in a Chevy, this was the first time I had run a Chevy engine in it too. Man it would scream, it just wouldn't corner.

stuff that worked was a mistake or an accident.

TOM: How big of an engine was it?

TOM: Well, that's the best kind.

DUFFY: Just a little 283. It was a 265 bored out to 283. On the West Coast here I never saw another sportscar with a Chevy engine in it before mine.

DUFFY: With the torsion bars this thing wouldn't get

Anyway, I ran the one race and I liked to kill myself. So I went back to the shop and wondered what the hell was wrong with this thing, why won't it handle any good anymore. I put a jack under one side of the frame and started jacking it up. I put a piece of paper under the tire, started jacking it up and pulling on the paper and when the paper slid out from under the tire, it only leaned a inch

Stu Hilborn's record holding B streamliner in the pits at El Mirage in the late '40s. Power is by a '34 Ford V8 with filled and milled heads, manifold by Eddie Miller ran four carburetors.
Three Stromberg E's and one double E Stromberg. Turned a two-way average of 145.640 mph.

and a half. I jacked up the frame a inch and a half and it would pick the wheel up. So that's when I went back to springs. Then I could jack it up six inches.

TOM: How long did it take you to build the Eliminator?

DUFFY: Probably six months. Paul and I both worked on it.

TOM: Why don't you go through that old VonNeuman story again.

DUFFY: Oh, we were up at Santa Barbara and the front starting grid is on a taxiway of some sort. It is wide enough for five cars and when you go into turn one, you skinny down into a little road that goes up behind some hangers and there are telephone poles, one on the right as you are going into the corner and one on the left as you are in the corner. That skinnies down at the start of the race and you can squeeze two cars through there, but up to the first telephone pole you can squeeze five cars, it's like driving into a funnel.

Anyway, we get the green flag and there is a little

A typical A-V8 roadster set up. This is a 21 stud early Ford V8 engine with polished heads, tall manifold complete with dual 97s and chromed velocity stacks.

The 1946 SCTA roadster record holder was Randy Shinn of Pasadena. Top speed was 128.66 mph. Car was also street driven.

Barney Navarro's A modified roadster. This 182-cubic-inch Ford V8-powered roadster qualified at the 1951 Bonneville Nationals with a speed of 125.050 mph. Barney was the man who designed and manufactured the Navarro speed equipment that was so popular in the early flathead days.

blown MG off to my right that I'm kind of watching with one eye and the telephone pole with the other. He's on my right and the pole is on my left, and I didn't want to crowd him because he would have gone into the snow fence and the pole. From the left side here comes the gray nose of VonNeuman's Testarosa.

He hit me right in the side at about a 45-degree angle, drove right into me, it was either me or the telephone pole, I guess. My left rear wheel rolled up on his car and that lifted the back end of my car on the two front wheels. The nose of his Ferrari was under my belly pan pushing me along so I just cranked it to the

Connie Wiedell's Cad-powered T roadster charged through the SCTA traps at 128 mph. Later turned 133.92 mph with a typhoon pushing him through the course. Connie belonged to the LA Gophers, an SCTA club.

right real hard and it came down on top of his Ferrari and just destroyed that thing from the firewall forward. Just smashed it.

I continued on for one lap feeling everything out and it felt fine. They didn't give me a black flag so I went on and I got fifth in that heat race. I went into the pits and started looked things over and the left header was bent a little bit and I don't know how this happened but the left door was pushed in about two inches from the steering wheel so it was a little close. I thought surely VanNeuman would come over and apologize for ramming me, but he didn't. I had a big hammer with rubber on one side and steel on the other, with a hot rod you carry all kinds of stuff like that. I'm hammering this door trying to get it away from the steering wheel a little bit and two of VanNeuman's pit men were standing around in the crowd, looking at the car. So I turned to my brother and said, "Ya know something Arnie, any asshole can go out and buy a new Ferrari, but these Model T doors are getting hard to come by." Well, I was the hot rodder black sheep of the whole thing anyway, and I beat a lot of them in my class, I always ran in the top five.

TOM: You probably had very little money invested compared to the rest of them.

DUFFY: Oh, yeah we had $2,500. I entered the Examiner Grand Prix knowing full well that I wasn't going to get into the race. There were a lot of big names and people all the way from Europe. Shelby had five cars there and Skip Hudson had a hand-built Maserati. I knew that I could go down there on

Bud Morelli, friend of Duffys, with Duff's '32 roadster in street trim. Headlights and windshield were removed and it was time to go racing.

This '23 T roadster looks like an old Ascot speedway car with its dual parallel leaf spring front end set up and half rear belly pan for drivers feet.

Not all trips through the lights were made without mishap. As can be seen in this photo, one '32 got on its head very hard. Driver's condition unknown.

Saturday and fill up with gas, get 25 gallons of gas, eight quarts of oil and a quart of brake fluid and run a couple a laps of practice. Then go out Sunday and get more gas and all the other stuff because all of it was in the can ya know. Then all my buddies and I would have pit passes and we could watch the race from the infield.

So I went out there and they had sudden death qualifying, and out of 52 cars, I qualified 15th fastest. Scared the hell out of me. I got a tape of the first lap of the race, I had a 16mm gun camera that I mounted on the roll bar. I thought well I got a button on the steering wheel and if anything happens in front of me, I'll push the button and get the action. It doesn't work that way, you're too busy trying to get the hell out of the way. I found out what you do, is as soon as the green flag drops, push the button and just let it run until you get your senses about you and can remember to turn the camera off. That Grand Prix, I got 11th overall and sixth in my class and won $600 some odd bucks.

TOM: Now when did that go-kart thing get going?

DUFFY: I was still running sporty cars, I was going to build a tube frame job, like a Formula car only with fenders. I had a model, that I carved out of hardwood and I wanted to get some pictures or information on the Kurtis car and I talked to this guy Bob Canan. I went over to Bob's house to look at some pictures. Bob had a bunch of pictures and I wanted to see what they were doing with their chassis. I remember I asked Frank what the balancing weight was on their car and he said 47 percent on the rear end. I had a A-frame that would pick up a locomotive, so I hooked some things in the frame at 47 percent, and I pulled the car up with a chain hoist and the front wheels were touching the ground, so I climbed in the front seat and the darn thing balanced out perfect with a half a tank of fuel in it.

So anyway, I went to Canan's house, and if I remember right he had built a little VW bug thing that he had out in the back. This is before the Manx came out with the body, this was a real crude looking thing. As I was walking out the back door, here's this little yellow engine sitting on his washing machine in his back room, and I asked, "What's this?"

He said, "It's a West Bend lawn mower engine for something Art Engles is building."

So, I went for a ride in his little VW bug around the Rose Bowl, I think it would do about 50 mph. Somehow I called Art, I don't know if I was going over there to find out about tube frames or what, but I went over to his shop and here's this kart sitting up on the bench. And I asked him, "What the hell is this?"

"Oh, just one of those little lawn mower engined things."

"That's pretty neat, would you mind if I built something like that?"

Engles said, "Nah, go right ahead. If you want to know anything about them just call me and I'll tell you."

So I got a look at the thing, and I went back to the shop, and I guess Roy was working out at Rubidux, and I was holding down the fort at GP in Monrovia. So I started building this little sucker out in the back room there. I called Art and got all the specs on it and Dick VanDeveere (Mooch) was a friend of mine, a salesman out on the road. I said, "Hey Mooch, I saw this real neat little cart, you shag the parts and I'll build two of them: one for your kid and one for me." So he shagged all the parts and I built two of them.

Roy was a stickler, he didn't want anyone working on their own equipment and their own cars during working hours and when he came up from Rubidux he asked what I was working on. And I told him that it was two little carts that I built during working hours, and he got hooked on it. So, Roy built two, one for him and one for old Rancid Ranny (Tom Noel).

I knew Marvin Patchen and Don Bobrick at the time through magazine articles and sporty cars. I was going down to the Rose Bowl and quarter midgets were heavy, kids would bring their quarter midgets down to the Rose Bowl, and we would go roundy round. I told Marvin and Don, "Why don't we get some rubber cones and set up a road race course instead of going roundy round all the time." So we did that and started running on the sporty car track and jeez, it really was fun.

Typical late '40s and early '50s street roadster engine set up. A 24 stud flathead engine, tall dual intake manifold, either Weiand or Thickstun. Ignition, either stock or a Lincoln Zephyr dual point conversion unit.

So, in the meantime people were wondering where we got our carts, and so we told them we make them. So many people stopped, we told them meet us here next week and we'll have all the parts for ya and it'll cost you $149. I drew a couple of plans on a brown paper shopping bag, I have pictures here and old 8mm movies when there were only 14 to 15 carts in the world. Someday, I'll put all of them on tape. Anyway, it just got bigger and bigger so we just started making them in the back room of the muffler shop and it got so big that we moved out to Irwindale and built the first kart track in the world.

TOM: Had the first nationals there, too.

DUFFY: Yeah.

TOM: How many championships over the years did the go-kart guys win. You won a few national championships didn't ya?

DUFFY: I built five cars. Gil Horstman, Tex Bell,

A shot from the roof of Dave Mitchell's muffler shop in Eagle Rock, California; hot rods everywhere you look.

The Nicholson brothers six-banger B roadster at El Mirage. Dyno Don Nicholson, as he would later be known, adjusts hood hold down straps prior to a quick run through the lights.

years. I took one of my spare innertubes, took the valve core out then took the powder out of it washed it out. I drilled a hole in the top of the fuel tank cap and put in a petcock, a regular little fuel petcock, and ran a fuel line from the petcock under my arm up in between my legs in the front and filled this innertube full of fuel and hooked the fuel line on to the valve stem. Left the thing down between my legs for about eight or nine laps and then on the straightaway I reached around and turned the petcock on and I slid this innertube underneath me and sat on it and squished all the fuel into the tank. It was a good thing that the fuel line didn't come off of the valve. But anyway, you should have heard the rumors that went around about what I had in that innertube, straight nitro and stuff. Anyway, we won all the national championships back there and came home. I built a cart for Bill "The Bone" Jefferies that weighed 45 pounds, and it looked like a regular Go-Kart 800. Unless you really got looking at, I didn't think ya needed a five-eighths bolt up there for the spindles, so I used a three-eighths bolt and I used .039 chrome moly tubing for the frame and I had it all heat treated.

Don Bobrick, Bill Jefferies and myself went back to Rockford. They asked how many laps we were running and I told them 10, because my car would go about 13 laps and then it was starving for fuel.

TOM: Which car was ya running then?

DUFFY: At the time it was the Konig two-cylinder water-cooled kart, and they assured me that they were going to run three heat races of 10 laps a piece. So when we got back there, they changed it to 15 laps. I decided to try something I had been joking about for

TOM: What was the stock wall thickness?

DUFFY: Oh, 085. Anyway, this thing, even

A sharp '29 roadster on '32 rails kicks up some El Mirage dust on its way down the course at an early SCTA lakes meet.

with the old vulcanized slicks that they used, weighed 45 pounds. I had Kenny Young back there in the Midwest, they were running carts that weighed 125-150 pounds, they looked like lounge chairs. I had Kenny put the thing under his arm and walk over to our pit area and he stopped and talked to guys, with the thing under his arm.

TOM: That's what was fun about the early karting days, really, because everyone was doing stuff to make it interesting, their own versions. I loved that part. Then when they got all that other stuff later, it was still fun but it was too serious.

DUFFY: I was building a FKE that didn't have a steering wheel. At one of the board meetings I asked, I knew what it meant, but I asked, "What does direct steering mean?" It meant you couldn't have a gear box, ya know? Cub Lions gets up and says, "Well, that means you can't run cables."

I asked, "Why not?"

"Well, they're dangerous."

So I asked, "Cub you got a boat at home don't ya."

"Yeah."

"Well, how do you steer that thing?"

"Well… "

"I know you have a pilots license, how do those controls on your airplane work?"

"Uhh… "

"Well, what do you mean they are dangerous?"

"Well, ya know what I mean."

"No, I don't know what ya mean. That's why I asked the question"

Bud Coffee was sitting next to me and he said, "What kind of steering do you have on your cart Duff?"

"Well, I'm trying a new thing. I ran a cable out through the axle out to the spindle and I left it at that." I think that Coffee went out into the Twilight Zone trying to figure out how the hell I was going to steer a car with a cable running through the axle.

Dave Mitchell's '29 roadster pickup truck under construction.

Dave Mitchell was not only a great car builder, as these photos show, but he was the first to use fiberglass to pack straight thru mufflers. His beautiful '29 roadster pickup was featured in HOT ROD MAGAZINE. Powered by a Olds V-8 engine and finished in great detail this little A was a real head-turner wherever it was driven.

Duff's channeled '32 roadster under construction. Shows how ya get 'em down in the weeds.

Mort Franciscas in his ohv and dual carburetor equipped four banger outfitted for the street. Note the stock A frame. Looks kinda naked minus the running board apron.

A very basic T-bodied four-banger modified. At the early post-war lakes meets it was kinda run what ya brung as long as it was safe.

TOM: Now when did you move down to Orange County?

DUFFY: Oh, I wanted to move down there anyway. I started going down Monday, Wednesday and Friday to try to set up. I bought Roy out of the muffler business and he moved up to Ventura, I was getting tired of the muffler thing anyway and I wanted to get into welding. I really enjoyed that and I was good at it and I still am.

Anyway, I set up a shop down there and went down there Monday, Wednesday and Friday and Bob would run the muffler shop, it was kind of slow up there anyways. Around comes the city to the guy that owned the property up there, and it was on a handshake, never on a deed or a contract. In 25 years, I paid $125 rent every month. The city came to him and asked would he like to sell the property and he said, "Well if Duff wants to stay, it's not for sale, if he wants to leave, I'll sell it." So, I heard all of this later. One day the old man came to me and asked if I was planning on leaving and I told him "no" and that was the end of that.

A little while later I get the word that the city has just condemned this property so I'd have to move within 90 days. In a case like that, they have to find a comparable location, but they couldn't find anything. So, I told them give me $10,000 and I'm outta here. They cut me a check for $10,000 and I got the word around that my muffler stuff was all for sale and Blair came out and said he would buy it. I gave him the key, told him he had to be out in 60 days and said, 'goodbye.' So then I went down to Costa Mesa and started my welding shop.

TOM: Now you just got a little shop of your own up there in Grants Pass, Oregon?

DUFFY: Well, not really. I do my own stuff. Build model airplanes. I have welded a few little goodies for guys, since I'd like to keep my hand in it a little bit.

A super neat little O Class streamliner was powered by a V4 Wisconsin engine. Driver was fully enclosed.

Duffy Livingstone, at the wheel of the mighty "Eliminator," blasts through turn two at the Goleta, California, road race course in the early '60s. Duff ran this car in Sports Car Club Of America competition for several years, finishing in the top five in class, proving that hot rodders can be road racers too.

AK MILLER

TOM: When was the first time you went to the dry lakes?

AK: The first time I went was 1934, and George White was running at Edwards Air Force Base. Of course in those days they used to team off in classes… 80-90, 90-100, and so on. The first ride I took in the '28 Chevy roadster turned 94 mph, so we got into the 90-100 class. That was my first ride, and I was only 14 years old! I had an approved helmet, which was an old leather thing. We had a roll bar, which was really the front end turned upside down. I got in and the old Chevy ran real strong and darn if I didn't get in the lead. I was really looking good, but about halfway through, the Chevy quit on me.

When you're in the lead, you can see. But when you're not in the lead, you can't see, and I knew that. So here they come by me… all these model A's and B's, they were driving by me. But then the big question is, when do I turn out, or go to the left? So the dust hadn't settled or anything, and I thought, I don't know where anybody is! So I finally started edging off to the left, and pretty soon when I come

out of the cloud, why here's a whole row of people rushing by. Of course, by that time I'm going about 65, and we had the best of brakes… two wheel brakes, you know. Rear ones. But you know, I had real good wooden wheels… excellent! The safety committee would check them for termites.

I got into that ride so young. I was just messing around with my brother, Zeke. And Larry, of course. Both of 'em were hot-rodders. But, Zeke had this thing, and I was helping him. I got up there, and he was going to drive. He got so nervous his foot was jumping up and down and his teeth were rattling; it was cold, but he was just scared.

I said, "What's the matter?"

And he said, "I don't feel good. Do you wanna drive?"

And I said, "Let me at that thing!" So that's when I put on the big helmet, and took off.

But, I'll never forget the first little bit of fright. Cars were lined up side-by-side for a long ways, and I was really gettin' it on. And about half way down there would be no cars. You know it was too far away. (This was runnin' in the speed trap.) So I'm going down, and hell no problem… I'm steering

The '32 roadster belonged to AK. This picture was shot at a motel in Temecula, California on the way to San Diego to street race Paul Schiefer of Schiefer Flywheel fame. AK's '32 ran 132 mph, Connie's T 128 mph!

AK Miller, as a boy, in the driver's seat of Connie Wiedell's Cadillac flathead V8-powered T roadster.

this puppy, and it's gotten up to about 90, or wherever it went, and then that side wind hit. And there I went. It was like skating land, off to the right. But I didn't panic too much, and I caught the thing before I got out of the trap.

We had the best of tires, you know. I think they were 450/21's. They were good rubbers. Sears Roebuck, the best they had. Guaranteed high speed!

AK Miller's '31 Chevrolet roadster. Powered by a 320-cubic-inch Buick Century straight-8 engine, this little beauty blew off many of the Ford V8 street racers, such as Don Blair, Jack McGrath and Manny Ayulo. AK's Chevy sleeper ran 118 mph at the lakes in those early days.

Tom: So, you were only 14, and you got really interested in it then?

AK: Oh sure. I had the fever long before that. But I was relegated to pulling the oil pans off of engines… down in the dirt, you know. I would take a screwdriver. I was great with a screwdriver. I could pull a pan off that Chevy four like nothin'. And I used to aim the oil squirters and I used to take the shims out of the lower end.

Tom: How much horsepower could you get out of one of those things?

AK: I've still got the old engine out here in the shop… the 3-port. I figure that puppy was getting somewhere between 125-150 horsepower.

Tom: Is that the same type of engine that Rufi ran?

AK: Exactly. The same as Rufi. And also Giovinine and Skivee. The pistons, I remember, were made by Egae. Chevys had the combustion chamber on top of the piston. They had about one inch of clearance. We'd install Durrant rods, which would lift 'em up maybe about half an inch. That'd really make 'em high. When you got through, you had some mean compression, about 7:1. You know they started out at about 5 or 5.5:1.

We used to be able to steal casing head gas. I lived right around Santa Fe Springs, which was an oil boom town. This was the drippin's, it had to be 60 octane. And knock… That stuff would ping, if you looked at it. Man, it was terrible. But, it'd run, and that's all we cared about. 'Cause gas at that time, as I recall, was pretty expensive… 10 cents a gallon.

In high school we really got serious on the Chevy. We purchased a Lee Chappel head, called the Tornado. That thing had ports you could stick your head in and out. Then we modified the oil sump, and we put on a Juet oil pump. And then we

The Road Runners club camp at one of the post-war SCTA lakes meets. Shade was hard to come by and the lake bed could get hot!

"Miller's Missile." AK in the cockpit of his 1951 Bonneville Modified '27 T roadster. The car weighed 1,560 pounds, had a 102-inch wheelbase and a 50-inch tread. Mercury engines were built by Taylor and Ryan. Nose graphics by Eldon Snapp. This car was tops in both C and B Classes, with speeds of 161.870 mph B Class and 172.744 mph in C class.

really threw some oil at the rods. We even opened up the bottom. They had a little tin plate. We'd open that puppy up, and could really throw a lot of oil in there. As I recall, we never did toss a rod in that Chevy.

Later on, of course, I got into the Chevy 6. I had this one all hunked up. This was just before the war. And there was a guy in our club (Road Runners) by the name of Bob McGee. And old Bob McGee had a beautiful '32. (That's the one that Scritchfield's got.) Anyway, Bob and I were the greatest of friends... and argue! Of course, I was Chevy, and Bob was Ford. Well, it finally got down to the nitty gritty, "Let's race!"

So we met on Sunday morning out by the Daley's olive orchard, out there in east Whittier. There's a nice long stretch with no side streets or nothing. Just the olive

Flathead City on the salt. The AK Miller pit area during his attempt to set three records in one morning. He was successful, but not before much thrashing and engine changes. Shown here in the foreground is the C Class flatmotor and behind it the V8 60. Engines were lifted in and out of the chassis with a 2x4. Check those flexie headers.

orchards there. So Bob and I took off on Sunday morning, and we had this race, and I took that Ford, with my little hot Chevy 6.

Pretty soon I looked up in to the rear-view mirror, and instead of Bob McGee, I saw some guy on a motorcycle. He looked like a real racer, 'cause he was laying down on the tanks. When I looked up he was wearin' a big star. He was a California Highway Patrolman. It turned out to be officer Ez Airheart. He said, "I've never seen a Chevy take a Ford... no way.

I heard about this race, and I had to come out and see it." I figured I was all done. What I told him was I was on an economy run, and was headin' for the beach... .

TOM: When did you switch to V8's? Who had the first A-V8 on this end of town?

AK: Some of the Stroker Club guys had the first ones. They had the little '29 A with a V8. I used to look for them too, with my little Chevy 6. Just for a little extra activity, you know. That was fun. Later on I discarded the Chevy 6. I took that thing out, and in its place I threw in a 320 Buick straight-8 Century motor. I think that thing cost $50 bucks, at that time, transmission and everything.

So I put that in the Chevy, and sure enough, it run. There's where I really got into the big street race scene with Don Blair and Manual Ayulo, and Jack LeGrand. We used to meet up and just go at it. I knew that those flatheads would either boil their guts out or drop something. I'd seen them drop a whole

Nellie Taylor in his very quick '32 roadster. Nellie was the Taylor of Taylor and Ryan Racing Engines from Whittier, California. This roadster ran 123+ mph.

cluster assembly right there in the street.

One night Don Blair said to me, "Gosh, almighty. You run this thing and run it... doesn't anything ever happen to it?"

I said, "No. Better not, otherwise I'd have to walk home."

TOM: What kind of a tranny were you running?

A very neat-looking Roots blower set-up on a 21-stud Ford flathead V8. Owner of this good-looking lakes car is unknown.

AK: A regular Buick. In them days, everybody had Lincoln gears in a Ford transmission. Those things were weak. I used to watch 'em, the sparks would fly. They would boil, the old flatheads could never cool too well. I'd just run 'em three or four times quick, and it'd blow up.

Do you remember Nick DeFahrity? We were always having top end races. DeFahrity had a little model A with a V8. It'd run about 121. Nag Nagley in our group had a '32, and was runnin' about 118 something. He says, "Hey, that guy isn't going to touch me on the streets."

So right behind the veterans hospital (at that time it was nothin' but beanfields), DeFahrity lost that thing, and he had just bought a brand new Chevy (about a '46 or '47 coupe), and it was sittin' there by the side of the road. And that darn roadster of his just went end over end, and hit that new car, and it killed him, of course. It was dead on. Of course, Nagley kept on, but they caught him. He learned how to grow potatoes at the honor farm.

I just talked to him the other day. He's busy building a 4-valve head for a Chevy.

TOM: The first time I met you guys was when

This 4-cylinder 1928 roadster, owned and driven by AK Miller, running only a SR Winfield carburetor, ran 94 mph at Muroc in 1934. It qualified for the fastest six-car drag race held that day.

Earl had his place down here on Greenley, and Nellie, and Ryan and the guys... .

AK: When they first started, they had a little garage. Larry, my brother, and I started Miller Brothers Automotive. We had a garage with quite a bit of room. So we invited Nellie and John Ryan to come on over to put their Chevy in our corner. That's how we got together.

Then later on up at Greenley, they had an L-shaped shop and they rented the rear. That's where Nellie and Johnny did their cars. They sponsored me too... my flathead engines, when I was runnin' my little roadster. That was my rear-engine one.

TOM: Nellie used to go like gang-busters in Orange County.

AK: Oh yeah... 120-121. His roadster on any given day was real good. Just to show you how serious this stuff was taken... in that garage, old dad was a devout flathead man. So here I am with a '32, and there's Nellie and John, there's nothing but a flathead. So here I am, and a guy gives me a small Buick straight-8. Dirty Dan. It was in good shape. So I say, "Yeah, I'll take it."

So I measured it up and figured I can put it in my '32. So I slipped that thing into the '32, and I found that I had to extend the hood just a little.

Rear-engine '29 Ford A V8. Notice the short driving compartment with gauges on the side panel. Several of these rear-engine set-ups were tried in the early Ford V8 days.

So of course, with the right sized Coca-Cola sign, I got the hood extended right. Everything looked good. That's when I put the independent suspension on it. Because I could never make the front end handle, and I thought that'd fix it. As it worked out, I hated the Ford front end, the dead axle. In those days I used to do a lot of cruising. I liked to get out on 395, you know how narrow it is, and I always like to run 85 or 90, whatever. Well, you couldn't do that with that dead axle. The thing would just bob and weave all over the darn place. I did everything… long springs, long shackles, short springs and shocks. Mounted 'em sideways, and up and down. And that Ford just would not handle. So, I thought I ought to fix that puppy, and I just threw that front end out, and drove the Chevy front end right under it… independent, see. Plus, it allowed me to stretch the wheelbase to set the Buick in it. Just perfect. And that did two things. It got me a real smooth car, and it got me a car I can run 150 mph down the road with, and the thing would just track beautiful. So I was well pleased with that.

And then the little engine, of course, all the Ford guys, Nellie, Johnny and all them, they got hot. Not

Vic Edelbrock Sr. standing between his '32 roadster (#59) and the '32 roadster (#60) belonging to Randy Shinn. Both cars are running for the Road Runners club.

only did they get mad, they threatened to do bodily harm. They were serious. So I said, "Well this thing will run reasonable." And they were cursing and said, "You dumb donkey. What's the matter with you. You know there isn't nothing that's going to touch a flathead."

So here comes Hank Negley. And Nellie says, "Here comes Nag. Are you tellin' me you're gonna run with his car?"

I says, "Yeah, if he shows up at Russetta, you better believe I will, 'cause I'm gonna be there."

I drove up to El Mirage, and sure enough there was Nagley, and they're tuning his neat little roadster. Well, I ran 118 somethin' my first run, and they could never touch it. So, I got the trophy. And then I

Unidentified Gopher club driver in this '29 roadster on '32 frame. The three-piece aluminum hood fit like a glove. El Mirage dry lake.

was in deep trouble. When I came home, it was all over. Somehow or other there was a $10 bet amongst all of 'em, and I had to take it. That hurt me.

It was switching engines, that really got 'em. But, I was always notorious about this. Let me take you back to my '32. I was one of the first guys to get an Oldsmobile OHV-V8 Rocket engine, when they first came out. I put that thing in, and I caught holy you know what.

They were always plotting against me. So in those days I had to make everything for the Oldsmobile, literally… you couldn't buy any of it. So, I made my own ignition, and then I made my own manifold with two carburetors, and did my hop up. Oh yeah, and they'd wear cams like crazy. So I went to see Harry Webber, and his dad had a Chevy four grind,

Don Waite stands beside his 257 cu. in. DeSoto V8-powered B Modified roadster during the 1953 Bonneville Nationals. The Waite-Bradshaw entry qualified with a strong one-way run of 191.59 mph, and then set a new two-way average speed of 187.667 mph.

that looked profile-wise just about what I thought I needed. But these things were tender on the cams. So I had Harry Webber grind this cam. And it had a pretty lazy profile, like a fuel pump would. It worked like a dream. That Oldsmobile would go to six grand. And of course a flathead would never see six grand.

After I did that little trick with the Oldsmobile, then I really got into trouble. Then, even my friend Doug Harrison, my co-driver on the Mexican road race, he called me nuts, crazy. He had a beautiful roadster.

I had this old homemade junk. And so finally one day Nellie Taylor told me it was a terrible thing I did. And why did I do crap like that when I've got a flathead? And, "I've given 'em to you… what more do you want?"

He says, "You're just nuts… you've gone crazy!"

I said, "Well it runs! That Oldsmobile runs pretty good."

"Are you kidding? Doug could take you down, and just blow your doors off."

I says, "Well, get 'em out."

So Doug and I went down on this old road, where Wayne Daley lived in amongst the orange orchards, (this was probably 1949).

Doug says, "Well, how are we gonna do this?"

I said, "I don't care."

You know, I had a Caddy transmission, and they're still playin' around with Fords. I said, "You better roll it."

He says, "Well you know the old flathead… if I roll it, it'll spin right on by that big hunk of iron.

I said, "Well, we'll try it."

And so we did a little roll start, and I just pumped that thing off. Just drove away from him. Then his face was extremely red, and he said, "Let's try it again, only this time let's try it a little slower."

So we did it again. Didn't make any difference. So I said, "Well, why don't you just start out in front,

Talk about a wild-looking coupe! This Talbot inline 6-cylinder three-window coupe was really a head-turner when Tommy Lee brought it to the lakes in the pre-war days. The 250 cu. in. engine moved the little coupe along at a 120 mph clip.

This roadster belonged to Wally Parks and was driven by AK Miller. The full racing cockpit cover was made from fabric stretched over forms and then doped, much like an airplane wing. The car ran four consecutive 123.45 mph runs in a row. Talk about consistency!

and I'll see where I really gain on you."

Before I ever got out of low gear, I was past that flathead. Those old Oldsmobiles run pretty strong. Well, that didn't endear me to that group. I was literally asked to leave. They really didn't want to see me in town. They didn't want me in their shop. And my dad teamed up with their guys. What a bastard I was, to shut down a Ford with a flathead! Especially when Nellie was giving 'em to me.

And I said, "Well, I just like to do something a little different that someone else doesn't do. If it's successful, don't knock it."

I was impressed with the Olds V8. My old buddy, Clinton Harris got the first one. He called me and said, "Come over here, I want you to drive this." I would just spin the wheels. I thought, "I gotta have one of these."

And it wasn't a week until the water hose was left off, and it just cooked one of 'em. So Clinton gave me that block. And then I went ahead and bought the rest of the stuff, and assembled my first Oldsmobile engine. That was a nice car.

Tom: When did you start running the Ford flathead V8's again?

AK: Even during that period, I was running one as I was sponsored by Nellie and he built my engine. Well, then I got into a whole different thing. I wanted to build a roadster. And I wanted to do it a little different.

That's when I started with my '27 T. I warmed that puppy up and got thinking about Bonneville. I thought, "Well, I'm gonna build this T and do something a little different."

That's the one that I made all my own independent suspension stuff for. Some guy gave me four Kurtis midget torsion bars, with the arms. I got to thinkin' this is what I need. So for the U-joints (we never had Thompson speed joints), I had to make 'em out of Ford U-joints, take the plate out of 'em. They worked fine, no trouble.

And for the front end, I did the divided type swing axle. I learned a lot from that. That's when I met this aerodynamics-type guy, named Art Ford. He used to come down. And he would say, "Well, if you really want to help yourself, you should do this and do that."

And so we rubber-sealed the belly pan on the roadster, so there was no air pumping loss. And we were able in one day, to set three records with that little car. With a little V8 60 first (A) class, and then the stock Ford next, and then the big one. We could

This photo, shot from the timing stand, shows a beautiful '29 roadster (#38) that the SCTA program said belonged to Richard Allen of the Lancers. Foreground modified roadster is AK Miller's ride, owned by Wally Parks. El Mirage, 1947.

change the engine in that thing, I think, in about 35 minutes.

TOM: Did the whole thing come out as a unit?

AK: Yeah. We just took that engine, and put a 2x4 under it, and two guys lifted and would slide it forward two inches, exhaust and everything. We had special headers. By the way, these were flex tubes. We used water cans… no radiator… we had two Jerry cans. We'd fill 'em full of water. They'd work fine. We knew the flatheads were gonna get hot. But how hot, was the only question.

TOM: Well, how hot did it get on a run down there?

AK: It didn't run bad at all. It was ample, one way. Then you got down there, and you sucked it out and put in about 4 gallons or so, and then make the return run. That system worked better than any radiator I ever run.

TOM: Were you runnin' all these records on gasoline?

AK: We never used any other fuel. We were never allowed to, so we ran regular old pump gasoline. I'll never forget when John Ryan and Dad and I had that thing down to change that engine. It was just two lousy bolts in the front on the motor mounts, and four in the back on the bell housing. Everything was snap, snap, and it was off, and we were ready to pull the engine. We left the headers right on, and they were hot still.

I remember one time, Art said, "You know we ought to try and get some ram into those carburetors." He got a thing off of an airplane he figured was pretty close to

Don Blair's blown modified at an early lakes meet. Check out the custom-formed hood piece. No lead, for sure.

what I would need. So, we sealed the carburetors. We put it right behind my head. So I was beginning to pick up speed with the 250 flathead and she's running down the course; the darn thing is running and reading pretty strong. I had a tachometer, so I knew I was running along pretty well. And all of a sudden it started like she was seizing up. And it was my doggone head getting into the air filter. Finally I thought about that and I cranked her over to the side, and the old flathead picked up. So, I set the record

AK Miller and Doc Ostich get some rays out on the salt while waiting to run AK's Oldsmobile-powered modified roadster. The Olds motor didn't do the number… only 168 mph.

SCTA starter Bob Higbee gives last minute instructions to Mal Hooper before turning the Shadoff Special loose on one of its record-setting runs.

The Shadoff Chrysler Special gets a push start (below) from engine builder Ray Brown Automotive's shop truck. With Mal Hooper at the controls, the Shadoff Special set an international two-way run of 236.36 mph on the Bonneville salt in 1953.

with that. I was telling Art, "I know that puppy is working."

So he said, "Let's put her on the big engine."

We did, and it wouldn't work. It just happened to work on that 250 cubic inch engine. Which, by the way, was a stock engine. Rebuilt for Jim Lindsay's truck I borrowed it.

I had told Jim, "You let me use that engine, Jim, and I'll give you a set of heads." I had a set of Western

Auto heads. They were iron. We put that on Jim Lindsay's engine and set the record. Jim was happy as all get out. So, we gave him the whole thing.

Then the little engine, that was the one that came from Ed Stewart. He had this little thing… it was a boat engine. He said, "Boy, I'd sure like to run this engine."

It ran over a hundred miles an hour for Kim Gench. It ran 142 mph. It was a

Willie Young poses with the Kenz-Leslie streamliner, which once again took home the big fast-time trophy with the fastest qualifying speed of 255.31 mph at the 1953 Bonneville Nationals.

An unidentified twin Hemi-Chrysler streamliner that was on hand for the 1952 Bonneville Nationals.

very good chassis. And Art Ford made me put it either way down on the ground or way up high. I figured putting it way down on the ground is gonna be a big problem. You know, no money or anything. So anyway, we decided to make it high. That was no problem. Everything came out fine. But it was certainly different from everyone else's. Because everyone else always dragged 'em on the ground.

TOM: I remember how high it looked, and thought there's got to be a reason for it.

AK: Yeah, well, that was it. Then we had the tonneau cover fit around my neck, like a tie. That was to keep the air out from inside the vehicle. We ran 176 on the big engine. The other one was 158 with the stock engine. By the way, that record stayed for a long time. Ray Brown, I think, finally got it. His engine, I know, had to be much better than the one I had. Although I

This very pretty '32 roadster was owned by Air Force Captain Chuck Adams. How about that truck front bumper?

You are looking at a $50 lakes modified roadster! Yes, that's right $50. As a project, AK Miller wanted to build a car from junk he had laying around. For instance, the flathead Caddy engine cost $5, the Columbia rearend was free, as was the 1923 Dodge roadster body. The radiator was from a P-38 WWII fighter plane, no charge. The wheels and tires were donated, and so it went. The result was a not-so-pretty car, but a 122 mph runner. Not too shabby for right after the war. AK would leave the car at the ranch near El Mirage between meets. Then on race weekend, he would take along a freshly charged battery and go racing.

AK Miller (driver) and Doug Harrison (navigator) at full song in the "Caballo" during the 1955 Mexican Road Race. Sponsored by HOT ROD MAGAZINE and manned by an all HOT ROD crew, the 339.83-cubic-inch Olds V8-powered roadster finished fifth in the large sports car class. The car was capable of 150 mph on the long Tehuantepec "freeway."

shouldn't say that. I don't know a thing about it. We just borrowed it from Ed Axle. He wanted us to try it.

TOM: When did you quit going to Bonneville regularly?

AK: After about six years. The end of the '50s. That's when I got involved in motorcycles and sports cars, and all that stuff. That took all my time. But those first five or six years, we gave Bonneville hell.

TOM: I had some pictures of the little low roadster you had with the little scoop and stuff on it, and then you had this long sharp aluminum cone.

AK Miller and his trick 4-wheel independent suspension modified roadster. The high stance was built in for aerodynamic reasons. It proved to be very successful. Just check the Bonneville Nationals record book from the early 1950s. AK's little needle nose had its share.

The Kenz-Leslie 777 twin-engine streamliner that was so dominant at the Bonneville Nationals during the early '50s.

AK: That was Wally Park's old car. That was a belly tank he put on the nose. He built the top out of canvas. I mean canvas, too! A regular old tent. Then he doped it, and got her tight. We never had any aluminum… we never had any money for that. These old belly tanks, I recall you could get 'em for next to nothin'.

TOM: I was surprised at how many front-engine belly tanks were runnin'. You know, the guy sits in the back, and the engine was up in the front

AK: Oh, yeah sure, a lot of that. Today they won't let you build a rear engine roadster. They lost a lot of 'em cause they would get light and pick up the front.

I don't know if you remember the terrible old beast that I had, the one with the Cad in the rear? It was a '23 Dodge roadster. It was the Road Runners, of course. We were battling for points against some club. We were getting beat, or close to it.

I said, "If I could get ahold of a certain item, I've got a Columbia and a Cad engine from a friend of mine that had a junk yard used to fix me up with 'em… if I could get a roadster… ."

Some guy said, "Well, I've got a

Bob Ward at the controls of Earl Evans' C Class lakester at El Mirage right after the war. This lakester turned 181.45 mph at the 1952 Bonneville Nationals.

An early lakes photo of Dick Kraft's modified roadster, nicknamed "The Bug." Notice the high-tech all chrome header pipe. Dick went on to be a star of the early drag racing scene in Southern California following WWII.

A very sleek unidentified tank is shown here on the dry lake bed. Note the used Indy 500 speedway tires run by most all the quick post-war cars. Spun aluminum wheel discs inboard and outboard minimize drag.

Harvey Haller and Frank Breene built this Chrysler V8-powered D lakester from a small side wing tank. The car turned an average speed of 209 mph. Doctor Nathan Ostich of jet car fame stands behind Harvey's missile. Bonneville, 1953.

roadster, but it's a Dodge."

So he gave me the Dodge, and it was the awfulest lookin' thing! Well then, for the nose, I used the old belly tank. For an engine it just had an old stock four. I used to leave the thing up at the goat farm, at El Mirage. And the goats used to ram into it all the time. I never took it home! Bring a battery,

fire it up, and put it in line. And it'd always get second or third. So, the points that we made there helped put the Road Runners over the top.

Everybody always used to moan about that thing.

Ed Metzer and AK Miller, fresh out of boot camp and home on leave, made it up to a lakes meet, uniform and all, before shipping overseas.

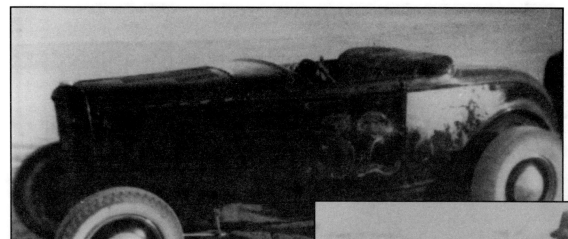

An unidentified '32 roadster with plenty of hood louvers, waiting in line at a pre-war lakes meet. It has the right number on the door for sure!

A rare picture of Vic Edelbrock Sr. moving his '32 roadster up in line, awaiting his turn to try the Purdy Brothers clocks at Muroc Dry Lake in 1940.

That puppy would lift up in the front. And we didn't have to go too fast... around 128 in that class. But, that thing would lift up just like a cobra. So I thought, "I'm scared of this."

So I put a big piece of iron I found (a big tractor flywheel) right on the front end. It must have weighed 200 pounds. And strapped her on there. Then she was pretty stable. Then the thing would go.

Later on in years, they put 300-400 pounds in front of those rear-engine roadsters, to keep them down. I was goin' in the right direction, but I didn't really have that much weight. Then again, I wasn't goin' 200 mph either. Those guys are getting up to 220-230 mph.

TOM: I don't understand how those guys run so fast at El Mirage, anymore. I mean it's not the smoothest surface that ever happened.

Don Blair's well-known lakes car, "The Goat." This supercharged Ford V8 flathead was one of the few cars running a blower at the lakes following WW II. Ran in the 136 mph class.

This car has been identified as the Spalding Brothers supercharged bobtail T modified. As shown here, the car is running a blown Riley ohv set-up on a Ford V8. The car was purchased by Don Blair and was known as "The Goat."

This beautiful C Class streamliner entered by Harold Post of Orange, California, turned the fastest qualifying speed in class at 217.62 mph at the 1952 Bonneville Nationals. Power was supplied by a Chrysler Firepower V8 engine.

AK: Yeah, I ride my motorcycle down there sometimes, and it's just a bone jarring experience.

TOM: They can run those cars up to 250. If they lost their brakes or didn't have their chutes only God knows how they would get stopped.

AK: Well, when we quit up there, I remember we used to have a lot of discussions about that. It was just absolutely unsafe, that place was... at any speed. Especially when you got roarin' about 150 and over. That was bad. And of course we lost a few guys up there.

TOM: You got goin' to Pike's Peak there, didn't you, and got all carried away?

AK: Well, yeah, that was in 1958.

Scotty himself fuels his Scotty Muffler Ardun-powered lakester during the 1953 Bonneville Nationals, just prior to setting a B Class record of 201.015 mph.

TOM: When did you guys build the Caballo?

AK: Well, that was in '53. I started in Mexico in '52. The first year, we got eighth place. But we were the only American car to finish in that class. All the Kurtis cars broke, Packards broke. Howard Hansen had some special stuff. The old Caballo would go, however, it had bad problems with the rear end. Every 300 miles my rear end would go. I was runnin' a '49-'50 Ford rear end. You only had 2 hours to work on your car. So we'd run into the pit and we'd get under there, grab the third section out. In the meanwhile, Ray Brock and the crew would round up a ring and pinion... we never brought any with us. We'd go to Mexico and get any gear we could get, and we'd pop that thing in and have her done in less than an hour. We only had one housing; so we just took the housing out and put the gears in, set it up, pre-loaded the pin... did everything.

This one time I remember, I pulled into Leon, and the rear end was sounding awful. And Doug says, "That's it. I'm not gonna go on. I'm gonna stay here."

Of course, Doug had his wife down there at the time. So, I couldn't blame him. So I said, "Well, I'm gonna go ahead and go."

He says, "What in the world are you gonna do when you're broke down there by the side of the road?"

Anyway, I was goin' along and that thing was

Low oil pressure required burning some midnight oil in Oaxaca to remedy the problem. Clem TeBow (left) and AK Miller doing the dirty work.

singin'. I found one place that was pretty good, and I was going along at about 115 mph. It was a tall gear, I recall.

Comin' up behind me I saw these doggone Lincolns. And of course it was Jack McGrath. He came right up behind me, and I'm punchin' that thing. He couldn't get around me. I towed him up to around a 120 somethin'. I was lookin' in the rear view mirror, and I see two other Lincolns. Well, they're way back there, and I never thought anything about it. Well, they accused me of skull duggery, of drafting, but heck that's racing. We really had fun in those days and I wouldn't trade them for anything. I got to go fast, scare myself a few times plus I met a lot of real neat guys. Would I do it all over again? All you have to do is ask.

The mighty Chet Herbert "Beast IV" set international 5-mile and 10-kilometer records, including the American 1-kilometer, 1-mile, 5-kilometer, 5-mile, 10-kilometer and 10-mile records. Driven by LeRoy Neumayer, the Hemi Chrysler V8-powered streamliner clocked a two-way average of 233.31 mph. These records were set at the International Record Trials sponsored by NHRA on the Bonneville salt, 1953.

JOHNNY PRICE

I first met John Price when I was selling ads for HOT ROD MAGAZINE, and he was working for Harry Weber, of Weber Cams & Flywheels. I'd been in talking to Harry about a little ad layout I'd made, and he said, "I want my shop foreman to take a look at this." He finds John Price, and of course I didn't know Johnny from a load of coal. We talked a little bit and somehow the conversation swung around to fishing.... We hit a common chord. From then on John and I have been great friends.

John is not just a pioneering hot rodder, as from the '30s and '40s. When the war came along he went into the Air Force as a P-38 pilot. Afterward he became a machinist and engineer, a great mechanic, and he's been at the Indy speedway with Mickey Thompson. In later years when I started building the first Volksrods, John got all excited and proceeded to build one. He put a little Porsche engine in it. I think it was the second nationals at Memphis, we decided to take both Volksrods. John's wife, Shirley, was determined to go along, five days each way. She was so enthusiastic after the trip that she wanted something bigger. I found a T touring in the L.A. Times classifieds and John built it with a four-banger engine using his own double overhead cams.

Semi-retired now, he has a machine shop at home. Walk out of the den right into the machine shop, it's really neat. He's got the mill and the lathe, all the

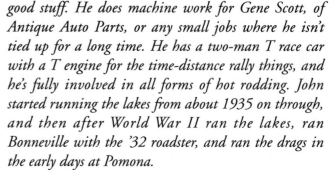

good stuff. He does machine work for Gene Scott, of Antique Auto Parts, or any small jobs where he isn't tied up for a long time. He has a two-man T race car with a T engine for the time-distance rally things, and he's fully involved in all forms of hot rodding. John started running the lakes from about 1935 on through, and then after World War II ran the lakes, ran Bonneville with the '32 roadster, and ran the drags in the early days at Pomona.

Back in 1957, I had bought a Volkswagon with that little rinky dink engine. I was very disappointed with the horsepower. At that time, Harry Weber was making a half-inch stroke crank, pistons, and a cam for the beetle engines. Price said to come on over after working hours. About 6:30, we whipped the engine out. John had to notch the case to make the extra room the rods would take up with the longer stroke, and we installed a cam and some pistons. Got it all back together, put it in the mighty Volkswagon and fired her up, at 3:00 in the morning. That's real hot rodding.

TOM: When did you first get started in this hot rod movement?

JOHN: Well, I think it was back when I was probably a sophomore in high school, in the mid-'30s. I went to... I forget which lakes it was, whether it was Muroc or Harpers, but anyhow I went with somebody. I went up there, and I became interested in it. I was driving at the time, but barely so. I lived up at the top of a hill in City Terrace at the time and we had no garage. I had bought this '26 Model T Roadster and took that apart piece by piece, carried it down in the basement—this was probably in late '34—and chopped up a frame. I think it was an Essex frame, I got parts from

Hero handler John in the early '50s with his '32 lakes roadster. Running for the LA Gophers, an SCTA club, John ran 118 mph at this lakes meet. Engine was a V-8 Ford flat motor, Wieand heads and manifold and a Weber F-4 cam.

another frame of some kind, cut everything apart and bolted the frame back together.

Then I chopped the body and made a one man modified, with the gas tank on the back, which was normal procedure, no turtle deck. I got it up on wheels, then took it apart and got it out of the basement piece by piece. Put it back together up on a place my dad had made to park the cars. Luckily, nobody stole it. Or maybe it was unlucky nobody stole it.

That was the first time I met Harry and Bill Weber. Harry was later Weber cams and flywheels. They came up, looked at the car and what I had to build it with, no welding equipment, they thought it was pretty good. I got the thing running, and I used to drive it back and forth to school. In auto shop, I made a set of headers for it. At that time, Weber Tool was down on Whiteside Avenue and all the guys—Nelly Taylor, Johnny Ryan—all of 'em used to hang around down there. One day I was down there bragging about the set of headers I made at school, and I was goosing the engine. I twisted the crankshaft off right in back of the flywheel. Of course I got all the scuttle-butt from the boys about how I should have built a Model A instead of a Model T. I was razzed about that for a long time. But I kept with the model Ts.

I don't know where I got the money to do this stuff. I think I was sweeping the floors at Weber Tool Company, for 10 cents an hour, for Harry and Bill Weber's old man. Anyway, I found a dual ignition Rajo. I used to babysit a family up on the hill, and the father had a wrecking yard out on Mission road. He used to give me a lot of the parts for this first car. So, anyway I got it together. Somebody talked me into taking it up to the lakes, maybe it was Nelly or Ryan, or all of them.

TOM: That was the only place you could go run legitimately and see how fast you were going.

JOHN: I don't know what year this was.

TOM: Do you remember what lake?

John's Fronty T modified at a lakes meet. A crew member holds the hood in place while John salutes the camera man.

JOHN: It could have been Rosamond, Muroc, El Mirage. Anyway, there was Bill Zaring, Ryan, Nelly, every damn one of them blew up, except ol' John's Model T. I run a little over 95 mph the first time I had it up there.

TOM: You run a Winfield carb?

JOHN: Yes it was, a Model M updraft carb.

TOM: That's hauling pretty good in those days.

JOHN: Well, yeah. The only four-cylinder that beat me, outside the model As and Bs, was Bob Rufi and his fabulous Chevy. So anyway, I was the hero around high school for a while. I kept with the Model T. In the meantime, Bill Weber built a modified roadster, and we turned the camshaft around in it and used a four-port intake and two-port exhaust on a Model A or B block. It was a flathead, a Winfield Redhead. We took it to the lakes and beat Bob Rufi's record. Second run Bill made with it, he blew the crankshaft clear out the bottom, it was laying on the lake bed. I don't know how many times we ran, but my fastest time up there with a Model T was 101.91

Bill Taylor's Model A roadster, using a solid steerable tow bar, towed John's roadster all the way to the lakes and back in 1935.

Little did Johnny Price (the one behind the wheel) know that not too long after this photo was taken he would be wearing the same type of helmet and goggles to fly P-38 fighter aircraft in the Big War. Johnny's 90.91mph Fronty T modified body is the rear half of a T touring. Engine is Fronty T with Ruckstell two-speed rear end. His co-pilot is "Wild Bill" Zaring of midget race car fame.

I kept that T for quite awhile. I even tried to run it at Southern Ascot. I was out of it for a little while, the war had come along, then after the war I had a '32 highboy with a flathead in it. In the meantime, we had started the cam business, Harry's dad had died, so we started the cam business together.

TOM: Did you guys do any street racing then?

JOHN: Not so much me, because I didn't have a transmission in the T, but I would go with Bill and Harry. Harry and I had been to the Montebello dance one night, we run onto this guy with a four-port Riley. We got to street racing, the cops got after us, we turned down a side street, this guy was ahead of us and he hit a dip in the intersection. His girlfriend flew through the top, didn't hurt anybody, and we got away from the cops. The four-port Riley beat us.

TOM: How many cars used to show up at those early lake meets?

JOHN: Oh, I can't tell you, quite a few more than you would think. The last one I recently went to there didn't seem to be quite so many cars.

TOM: What timing associations were sanctioning?

JOHN: SCTA and Bell.

TOM: Let's see, SCTA started in '39.

JOHN: I belonged to that and the Gophers, in fact, I was a charter member in the Gophers.

TOM: Who all was in that?

JOHN: Bill and Harry Weber, Nellie Taylor, Johnny Ryan, Mitch Rodriguez, Stan Sherrel, Bill Zarring. We used to meet in his garage all the time. A lot of them I can't remember.

TOM: Timmerman belonged to the Gophers later didn't he? He was running a Gopher plate when I first met him.

JOHN: Yeah, I think he did. Oh, and Jack McGrath was there and maybe Manual Ayulo. There was a bunch of them that became famous in the racing business.

TOM: How did you get the name Gophers?

JOHN: When we were chartering this thing, we kept thinking of names and somebody brought up Gophers. The rest of us had no idea what the heck that had to do with hot rodding, and the guy said, "Pass one and go for another." So, that's how it came to be.

TOM: I run that Gopher plate on my '40, and a lot of guys ask what's the Gophers? They always say it doesn't make sense, and I tell them it does.

TOM: When did you go to work with Harry?

JOHN: I went to work for Weber Tool Company right after I got out of the service in '45. I used to sweep floors for the old man way back before that for 10 cents an hour.

TOM: What's the bit about the tow bar?

JOHN: One time Bill Taylor, of Indy fame, midget fame, whatever you want to call it, took me up to one of the lakes. We had a tow bar, but I had to steer the thing. We'd get to a hill, and I'd fire the T up and push him over the hills. We got up there OK, but coming home the traffic was heavy. Sunday afternoon. I say heavy, that's a joke, compared to now. He went to pass someone, and I guess he forgot I was back there. He pulled in quick, leaving me out there on the wrong side of the road and this car is coming and I had nowhere to go. Luckily the guy I was meeting had sense enough to get off the road, but it was a little puckering I tell you.

Another time Weber Tool Company moved from Whiteside Avenue over to Eastern Avenue. Not too far from where Offenhauser is now. I was towing the T over to the other shop. Supposedly I had a steerable tow bar on it. As I was going over Eastern Avenue the T came off the tow bar. I looked out and here goes my T right by me. Luckily it turned left, went over the bank, and down on to the Southern Pacific Railroad tracks. I was by myself and I had a hell of a time getting the thing off. I managed to get it free and got a long rope and towed it back up on the road. I guess it was vibrant youth and 100 percent dumb luck most of the time.

TOM: You were drag racing there for a while, weren't you?

JOHN: I had a '32 highboy, that was when Harry started the cam business and he sorta sponsored the car for me. It was a nice highboy, nothing was moved, it had the full transmission in it, plus a quick change. I used to run at Pomona drags most of the time because that was closest. In those days, I couldn't afford to travel very much. I had a flathead, it was one-half by 3 5/16. I'd burn anywhere from 20 to 30 percent nitro, I set a record with that at Pomona for a year at 125.86 in the quarter. It was a B Roadster. I kept that for a long time, I made all the runs I could. In fact, there are trophies on the shelf up there from different places. Then I sorta got out of it. I ran that same roadster at Bonneville in 1953, C Roadster Class, Weber Cam Special, 136.15. I was on my fourth engine. You should richen the mixture when the heat pulls the moisture out of the salt. I was going the wrong way, until, I think it was Granatelli, that gave me the idea. Told me I was going the wrong way, so I richened up, but still wasn't rich enough. I thought I had the record in my class until somebody

THE P-38 THING

I've known Johnny Price for several decades, most everyone connected with racing knows him. Let me fill you in on the P-38 thing. During World War II, John was flying P-38's out of North Africa, going north over the Mediterranean and up through Italy. After one mission deep into Nazi-held territory, he was flying tail-end-Charley in formation, returning to Africa. Without warning, an ME 109 jumped his tail and dropped a 20mm caliber into the P-38 cockpit, exploding the instrument panel. The explosion caused John to lose one eye, and there was so much blood he couldn't see out of the other. He passed out, to be awakened by water spray.

Apparently he had fallen out of formation, but the plane had descended gently and was flying itself just at wavetop height over the sea. Props cutting into the water were throwing spray into the disintegrated cockpit, which is what awakened John. He was still flying blind, literally, with no instruments to tell direction, or anything else.

By a stroke of luck, another flight of P-38's overhead happened to see John's plane on the deck. One pilot dropped down to see what the matter was, to discover that John was in bad shape. He radioed to John, got a nod of agreement, and led John home to North Africa, barely above the water.

The airbase was right on the shoreline in Africa, the other pilot lined John up with the field and talked him onto the runway. John still could see practically nothing. Just thought I'd share that little aside, to give you an idea of how competitive this Johnny Price really is.

—Tex Smith

came down from the Ozarks someplace with a Dodge Red Ram. He beat me, he turned 140 or something. That was the only time I ever ran at Bonneville.

TOM: You were with the railroad or something when you went into the service weren't you?

JOHN: Yes, I was a brakeman on the Santa Fe and was also tied up with midgets at that time with Bill Zaring. When I was working the extra board on the

Johnny Price in his narrowed '26 T modified. Power was supplied by a Model T block, T counter balanced crankshaft, BB Rajo head, Fronty side drive, and a Stutz-Bearcat dual ignition. Rear end was a Ruckstell two-speed unit. In 1935, John ran 101.91 mph at Muroc Dry Lake, it is now known as Edwards Air Force Base.

railroad I'd try to time my trips so I could lay over in San Diego and go to Balboa Stadium to see the midgets. That's what got me started in the midget thing.

TOM: You were in the Air Corps flying P-38s?

JOHN: Yes. *(See sidebar)* One day I dead-headed a P-38 down to Long Beach and I ran into Rex Mays in the ready room. We got to talking, and I told him what little midget experience I had, and he says, after the war look him up. After the war, I didn't have to look him up, he found me. We lived at La Cienega Aerodrome at the time, right across from Pete Navotne's garage. Everybody hung out at Pete's garage. So I met Rex again, this was around '45 or '46. He said he had a spot open on the pit crew, if I wanted to run the crew. I said fine. Joe Garson was driving, we had four firsts. Well, maybe I'm wrong on that, I don't remember if it was four or 44. Anyway Joe was driving one car and Mel Hanson, when he was in town, would drive the other one. Rex would drive once in a while, but his wife would get so upset when he drove the midget. Rex didn't really like midgets, he said his ass was too close to the ground, he didn't really like 'em. He'd go out and qualify some good times and then put somebody else in. He did a pretty good job in it.

I met a lot of nice people there, including Frank Sinatra. I was laying under a car one day and this guy drove his Cadillac convertible in. I heard him tell Pete he wanted to make the thing go fast. Pete says, "see that kid laying on the creeper under that car, go over and talk to him." The guy comes over and kicks my feet and says, "Pete told

me to come over and talk to you." So I crawl out from under the car and face to face with string bean Sinatra. He says, "Pete tells me you can make this thing run fast." I says, "how much money you want to spend on it?" He says, "Money's no object, I just wanna make it run fast." So I told him what I was gonna do on it, and he says, "I don't know anything about it, just do what you have to do, and make it run fast." I put on a set of Edmunds heads, a manifold with dual carburetion, changed the curve in the ignition, then that thing set around for at least two months. My first wife used to go sit in it. In fact, I took her around the block once.

He finally come in one day, and he says, "You get the car finished, kid?" I think I was probably as old as he was. I don't know how old Sinatra is, maybe I'm older. Anyway, he says, "Does it run?" I says, "I think it runs pretty good." He says, "let's go for a ride, kid." I never had a wilder ride in my life, I tell ya. He brings it back, pays Pete off, and says, "Kid ya did a good job, I love it. There's one thing, any time I bring that thing in here, you're gonna work on it." I left Pete's and I went to work for the county for a little while, where I was in charge of all maintenance on the iron lungs. In the meantime, Harry Weber got talked into the cam business by Phil Wieand. We used to grind Whizzer cams, just on the side. Phil talked Harry into going in the cam business, and I went back to work with Weber. I was vice president of the company for 20 some odd years. Then he moved down to Santa Ana, and I was living in Arcadia at the time.

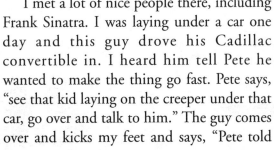

Gopher Club member Sonny Granagan and friend push their Model A roadster to the starting line.

TOM: Tell me about your session with Micky Thompson at the speedway.

JOHN: Oh, I was going to get to that a little bit later. Anyway, I worked with Harry until he went to Santa Ana. So I called Mickey one day and asked if he could use me. He used to come into Weber cams where I used to run his engines on the dyno all the time. I went to work for him. He bought one of our old cam grinders, and I started grinding cams. Pontiac would send us specs, and I would make the masters and grind them. If they didn't work, I would add to them or take out of them. It all worked out pretty good, Mickey and I got along fine. Luckiest man in the whole world. I know one morning, I was in there early and he came in with a little black satchel and he said, "Come in the office, John." So, I went in and I forget what he had, 10 or 12 thousand dollars. He says, "You know what I'm going to do, I'm going to buy the spot next door." And by golly he did, and we built a building on it. That's where we built the race cars. That was in Long Beach. I think the store faced Anaheim Boulevard. I stayed with him for about six years.

We went to the Speedway in '63. Two cars weren't enough, he had to have four, which was fine. Two of them were little wheel cars, and two of them were big wheel cars. I think we ended up, I can't remember who drove it, oh—Dwayne Carter. I think he finished seventh if I remember, which was pretty damn good. We had two cars that got in the race, I forget what the other one finished. Anyway, I stayed with Mickey a little while after that.

TOM: I was there that year, I remember you got all ticked off for some reason and left before the race.

JOHN: Cosworth was the guy's name, and the last day of qualifying we damn near came to blows. I would have hit that Englishman in the mouth one night, but Fritz's wife grabbed me and calmed me down a little bit. I just packed all my stuff up and came home. I departed from Mickey, and that was about the end of my racing. Did I mention tuning for Sam Hanks when he was in Alhambra?

TOM: Then we did the Volsrod thing, followed by that T Touring I found in the *L.A. Times* classifieds.

Bill Warth's beautiful early lakes streamliner of the 1930's, with a Ford four-cylinder. This car later was purchased by Stuart Hilborn.

An unidentified tail job gets the once over from spectators as it waits in the starting line.

That was a '24 tub, all steel, for $1,800.

JOHN: Yeah, I built that thing from the frame up. It has a double overhead cam head on a Model T block and a Model A crank. It is full pressure oiled with counter balances. It's a good runner. I had a stick in at first but I have a bad hip and the clutch was too much, so I put an automatic in it. That worked out great. Anyway, I joined this Model T club, and they have these rallies once a year, so I built a replica of a '21 Morton and Breck Two-Man Race car, with a Rajo in it. Anyway, that's worked out good. It'll run all day long.

One other thing that I want to get in this story. We were up to the street rod run at Kernville, and I run into Magoo. He says to one of his buddies, I can't remember who, he says, "John Price has got the only real built up from scratch street rod here." That made me feel real good.

Starting line scene of an early dry lakes meet. Note the elaborate timing stand, no shade for the phone man.

BOB RUFI

Bob Rufi began racing on the dry lakes of Southern California in 1937. He and friend Charlie Spurgin ran a four-cylinder Chevy-powered modified that was one of the fastest cars in its class. When the Southern California Timing Association announced there would be a streamliner division in 1938, Rufi and Spurgin added a canvas tail to the modified and competed in the new class. The slicked-up modified set a streamliner record with a two-way average of 115 mph.

Despite the success of the streamlined modified, Bob decided to build an all new race car. Armed with a book from the public library titled *Speed and How to Attain It*, by Ricardo, and with Ernie McAfee's guidance on chassis construction, Bob began building a new streamliner.

The streamliner's first competitive event was the season opener at Harper Dry Lake in May of 1940. Bob qualified the car with a pass of 136 mph, and after a little tweaking ran 137 mph. Leaning out the carburetors two notches and spinning the little four banger 5,000 rpm resulted in the historic 143.54 mph pass. A 137 mph back-up run gave Bob a new streamliner record with a two-way average of 140 mph.

A number of things were changed on the car for subsequent meets. Several different modifications were tried, including pants over the rear wheels. Unfortunately most of the tinkering actually made the car slower. However one promising change was the installation of 3.08 rear gears. Bob calculated that if the engine would pull 5,000 rpm with the taller gears, that would equate to 150 mph. On one run, the engine did pull the five grand, but it detonated so severely that the head broke, ending the attempt to raise his own record.

Even though he was not able to break the record set at the season's first event, Bob, was the SCTA points champion for 1940 going into the last meet of the season. That's when disaster struck. The season finale at Harper was held on a cold and overcast November day. As he accelerated down the wet course the car got loose, turned sideways and flipped, landing upside down. Although the chassis held together remarkably well, Bob sustained injuries. He was pulled from the car and taken to the hospital. Considering there was no roll bar and these were the days before helmets, Bob was lucky not to have been hurt more severely.

After his release from the hospital Rufi decided his

Bob helped Jack Rose get his injured race car home from the roadster races in Santa Maria. All the parts knocked off by a new driver were retrieved, tossed in the driver's seat, and reattached for the following weekend's racing.

Charlie Spurgin turned his car over on Pico Boulevard and destroyed the body, so he turned what was left into a speedster. Worked just fine for towing Bob in the two man.

racing days were over. In 1941, he sold the car for $100. The new owners of the car ran the lakes briefly after World War II, then a legend in American hot rodding disappeared.

TOM: You got into hot rodding about 1937 with a car that was originally built to run roadster races, right?

BOB: Yep.

TOM: That was a Chevrolet-powered car?

BOB: Yeah, the only engine I ever used was a four-cylinder Chevy. We always used a 1925 block because the center main bearing web wasn't cut out for the ignition like the '26 was. The '26 had the ignition on the side, it penetrated the center main bearing web to get a gear down by the camshaft.

A dapper Tommy Lee waits to make a pass across the lake bed in his Bugatti. Harper Dry Lake, 1938.

TOM: The '25 ran the distributor and the oil pump off the generator, right?

BOB: Yeah.

TOM: Did you build that first car?

BOB: Yes, I built the entire thing. Had the frame rails welded up and had the radiator built, I made the radiator shell out of a Studebaker gas tank that had a ridge on it and then we cut a heart shaped hole in the front. I think we made the grille insert out of a Ford V8 piece. We cut it and put it in so

Lyndal Dills (left) worked for Lockheed Aircraft Company. He taught Bob how to form the aluminum body panels for the new streamliner. The body of the new car can be seen in the background, upside down in its construction cradle.

we would have some straight chrome strips, around the edge of that heart shaped hole we bent some mild steel and chrome plated it for trim. My buddy Art Robbins worked at a junk yard, and he got me most of the stuff for the car.

TOM: How many years did you run that car?

BOB: A couple of years I guess. Then Chuck Spurgin and I wanted to go to Oregon, we were single and we were going to drive up to Oregon, we were going to make a two-man car for the trip. We went up to Decker Canyon and pulled a 1924 Dodge out of the brush and used the frame rails and the body and modified it to make a two man. We built that out of the pieces of the one-man.

Using a homemade polisher, Bob buffs the aluminum body of the new streamliner. The car's skin was shaped over plywood patterns, the formed panels that made up the body were then attached to frame mounted hoops made of electrical conduit.

TOM: Did you use the same Chevy engine?

BOB: Yeah, we used the same engine because it ran good. In fact, when it was still a one man, we started out right near Pico and Robinson and put a gallon of fuel in it, this was early one Sunday morning, I think we even made a muffler for it, and drove 'til it ran out of gas, which was up near Decker Canyon. We got 33 miles to the gallon.

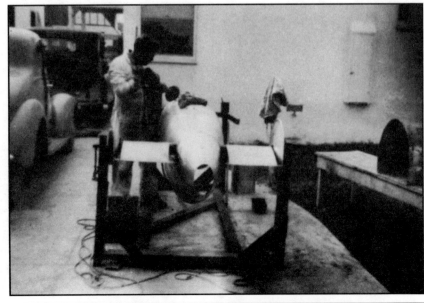

Tom: Did that have Winfield carburetors on it?

Bob: Yeah, two updrafts.

Tom: What was that chassis made of?

Bob: On that car the frame rails were four-cylinder Chevy rails, and they were welded up by a guy in Glendale, he filled the holes in 'em too.

Tom: So you turned all of those pieces into the two man?

Bob: Yeah, we took all of the pieces and built the two man. This two man was 50 inches wide, and it had the Chevy engine with a B crank and Model A rods. The compression was 9 or 10 to 1. It had an Olds three-port head.

Tom: Did that car get raced or was it just a street car?

Poking out of the tail of the 'liner was the Eddie Miller exhaust system. Bob still has header and pipe, the only parts of the car that remain. Rear axle fairing was used to create down force.

Bob: It was raced at the lakes. We never did race it on the street or take it to Oregon, we never got enough money together. Both of us were responsible for our parents so there wasn't much left. You know,

Bob and Charlie Spurgin modified their two-man car to run in the streamliner class by adding a tail built of wood and muslin. The revamped car was the first to run SCTA's streamliner class.

The shape of Bob Rufi's streamliner was suggested by a book from the public library. According to the text, the widest point on the car should be a third of the overall length from the front. That's where Bob sat.

Chuck and I have been friends since we were 10 years old. We went to the same grade school. We used to take the wheels off our wagons, grease 'em up then take 'em up this one steep hill and race each other down.

TOM: When did you start construction on the streamliner?

BOB: That was about, well we set the record in '40, but we ran in '39, and between '39 and '40 I modified it. So it must of been 1938 when I started.

TOM: The chassis of that car was made out of electrical conduit, right?

BOB: Yes, I think it was two-inch ID, something like that.

TOM: You used a library book to help design the car,

was that the book that gave you the idea for the tear drop body shape?

BOB: I don't know if it was that book or another book that talked about streamlining. Anyway, one of 'em said that the widest point on a streamlined car should be a third of the distance back from the nose. That worked out so if I sat in the front, I was the widest part, about two feet wide, and everything else would be tapered from there on back.

TOM: That car was rigid, no suspension?

BOB: Ernie McAfee was the first guy to do that. His car was a springless wonder, too. The frame tubes went into holes in the rear axle housing, in the front the tubes were welded to a Model A front axle. Something else Ernie did for me was to sell me the patterns to cast the side drive that ran the ignition on that engine. Jim Travers' dad had a casting shop, so

Jim took the patterns down to his dad's shop and cast 'em. I paid Ernie two dollars for those patterns.

TOM: And all the aluminum for the skin came from Douglas Aircraft surplus sales?

BOB: Yeah, they called it cash sales in those days. I bought 4- x 8-foot sheets. I built the streamliner in a cradle that I built and used a building instrument so that I knew that everything was level where the axles were set, so the wheels would all be the same height. I set the front axle, which was a new Model A Ford axle, and the Chevy rear end in there and drilled some holes in the Chevy housing as close as I could get it to the third member, then welded the tubes to the housing. In those days, we kind of reciprocated with everything. Tony Rocha was the man who welded it together, his garage was falling down so I repaired his garage for him and he welded the car.

The last lakes meet of 1940 ended Bob's racing career. The streamliner got sideways on the soggy Harper lake bed and flipped. Considering the lack of a roll bar, the car held up remarkably well.

TOM: You were a carpenter by trade?

BOB: Yeah.

TOM: So, he put the chassis together for you, and did he build the hoops that gave the body its form too?

The Rufi-Spurgin two-man modified The car was dubbed the chicken coop because of the wood and muslin tail added to make the modified into a streamliner.

The first run on alcohol took place on Lincoln Boulevard behind Mines Field, now the sight of Los Angles International Airport. Note the radiator inlet in the nose has been taped off to build some heat in the alcohol fueled engine.

multiple disc clutch. I'd hang on to a rope and Chuck would pull me up to speed, then I'd clutch it off and go.

TOM: Did the streamliner run a Tornado head at one time?

BOB: No, I bent all of those, I made plywood patterns. I'll tell you what I did to get the shape of the body, I used parting bead, which separated house windows when they went up and down in the double hung window, a three-eighths by three-quarter inch flexible piece of wood. I used that, I figured out how wide a place I needed for my feet, then widened out to two feet wide where I sat, then 11 inches wide at the rear end. Then I bent the parting bead and fastened it and measured the distances and made the hoops, the framework that the skin fastened to. The section on the bottom, where my butt sat, was round, the top section of the body was elongated like an egg, to have room for my head

TOM: Didn't Eddie Miller build the exhaust system for the car?

BOB: Yeah, that's the only piece I've got left of the car, I've still got the exhaust system. It's beautiful.

TOM: As I recall that car ran without a transmission?

BOB: Yeah, it just had a Model A

Bob underway on Lincoln Boulevard passing the tow car. Openings in the body, just behind the rear wheels, vent air passing through the radiator.

BOB: No, the only head I ever used was an Olds three-port. I used a Sears Roebuck drill and a Sears Roebuck grinder stone to open up the intake ports. I used the four-cylinder Chevy because it was cheap, I didn't have any money, but I used the three-port Olds head because it had a better exhaust. After we'd been running the car for a while I pulled the individual carburetors, that book, *Speed And How to Attain It,* had a paragraph in it that said the closer you could get the venturi to the intake valve the better off you were because there was a shorter column of air to start off.

So I said to myself, "What the hell, I can put the carburetors right on the head." I didn't need any manifold, so I took some 1 7/8-inch tubing and

brazed a flange on there that would accept a Winfield bowl and then two dump tubes, one for the intermediate and one for the high speed, and ran those across the venturi with a slight angle so that would make the vacuum to pull the gas out of the carburetor. They didn't have any idle circuits, I wasn't interested in idling anyway. It would run about 60 mph at start up. So anyway, that was the reason I built the carburetors like that. We put the twin carburetors on and ran the thing out back of Mines Field to see if they would work, then we took it up to the lakes. We used alcohol by the way. I keep going back to that book, it had a formula in there for the alcohol. We ran 10 percent gas, 10 percent benzol and 8 percent alcohol and about a cup of acetone.

Tom: What kind of compression were you running?

Bob: The streamliner had 15:1. Now, here's another interesting point. Down on Main Street in L.A. there was an aircraft junk yard. I went in there and found these connecting rods that were made out of billet steel, they were for an OX5 aircraft engine. I bought the con rods and the caps and the bolts for 35 cents apiece. I put those in the engine and unknowingly, I knew that they were longer, but I was one of the first guys to use longer con rods to get a better rod angle. They were about three-quarter-inch longer I think.

Tom: Let's go back to the day you set the record.

Bob: Well, on Saturday it was a clear day and this was the first time I had a tachometer in the car, and so I took it out and opened it up and it read 5,000. Well, with the gear ratio the car had, that worked out to be 140 mph. So I thought there was something wrong with the tach. Then it started to rain so we had to pull off the lake and set up camp. I didn't think we would even run, because the lake bed was really wet, but the wind blew all night and dried the lake out so it was good and hard. So we went out and got in line. The first time we went down, I think we went down at 136 or 137 mph. After that run all I did was fiddle with the carburetors, I didn't even open the hood all the way, I just lifted it just far enough to lean it out two notches on each side, and we did 143 mph.

Bob's streamliner record stood for 10 years. It was finally broken in 1950 with this car driven by Stu Hilborn.

In attempt to coax more speed out of the little 'liner, Bob and Eddie Miller built pants for the rear wheels. Though they looked zoomie, the car didn't go as fast with them as without.

TOM: Did you get waved off the course on that record run?

BOB: Well, let me tell you about that wave off. We went down on a record run, we went down at 143 mph and went out and made a big circle and came back to make a return run, and Art Tilton, who was secretary of the SCTA, gave me a red flag. I ignored it and went onto the course. I remember going halfway through the course and thinking the timer could be haywire so I shut it off and Crocker got me at 137 mph with the engine off and coasting the last half. When I threw the clutch out, the nut on the front of the driveshaft came off, I hadn't put a cotter pin in it, and when it came off it jammed that multiple disc clutch. I couldn't run the car again because I couldn't get it started without that clutch working. So, we accepted the 137 even though we had coasted. The car was running 5,200 going back just like it did going down, which was 143 mph. The next race we did 139 mph with it but I had taken off the carburetors that I had made and put some that Duke Hallock had made on it. I liked the system Duke had for mixing the alcohol and the air.

TOM: Weren't you on a 150 mph pass when the engine let go?

BOB: We put in a tall gear, 3.08s. We were on the course, I think it was a record run, and according to the tach we were going 150 mph, but it got to detonating so I had to back off. When I got out of it, it quit detonating but I was still on the course so I gave it a little more throttle and it started to detonate again and this time it broke the head. The left front corner of the head broke clear off.

TOM: Other than that episode, was the engine pretty reliable?

To extend valve spring life, the pushrods were removed from the engine between events. Here Bob pushes down on the valves while Jim Travers (kneeling) installs the pushrods.

BOB: Well, that engine with the OX5 rods in it, we never had a bit of trouble. One of the engines in the modified, I can't remember if it was in the one man or the two man, broke a con rod. I think the reason the rod broke was the intake rocker arm broke first and then the intake valve wouldn't open so it pulled the rod. But other than that, they were just great. Never broke

TOM: Was the engine in the streamliner full pressure?

BOB: Yeah, the shaft was drilled by Paul Frome, Jack Taylor used to put my bearings in. Jack Taylor and Paul Frome shared a shop. Frome was the guy who built the engine for Rex Mays engine when that rocker arm beat all the Miller's, Rex had the championship that year.

TOM: You tried some pants over the rear wheels at one time, how'd that work?

Out of curiosity, Rufi and Spurgin decided to see how far the modified would go on one gallon of gas. An impromptu economy run netted 33 mpg.

BOB: Wish I'd never done it. They weren't solid enough. I made the framework, Eddie Miller built the pants themselves.

TOM: Tell the story about you running the streamliner out by Mines Field.

Bob's record setting streamliner weighed in at 950 pounds, with Rufi behind the wheel. Tires were 7:00-16 Speedways, aluminum wheel covers were surplus WW I Jenny aircraft items.

Chevy four-cylinder was equipped with an Olds three-port head, Ford Model B crank, Winfield cam, Jewett oil pump, and surplus military aircraft engine connecting rods. Eddie Miller built the exhaust system, Rufi built the carburetors that featured Winfield float bowls and changeable venturi.

BOB: The first time we ran the car on alcohol we went out behind Mines Field (now Los Angles International Airport) on Lincoln Boulevard to see if the alcohol carbs would work. The engine had been run on gasoline, but we wanted to see how the alcohol system worked. With no idle systems, the slowest the car would run was 60 or 70 mph. Anyway, as I was going down Lincoln, a motorcycle cop going the opposite way spotted me, but I didn't see him. He made a U-turn, pulled his hat down, and took off after me. The guys in the push car saw him, but I didn't know I was being chased. I shut down, and was climbing out of the car when the cop pulled up. He looked the car over, and said he ought to write me a hell of a ticket, but he didn't know how to describe the car. He said if I promised to never run that thing on the street again, he'd let me off. I promised.

Bob (left) and Ralph Schenck stand along side their lakes modifieds. Ralph is credited as being the first engine builder to put a Ford crankshaft in a Chevy block.

Tom: Not only did you set the streamliner record in 1940, but you were the SCTA points champ as well.

Bob: Yeah, I set the record then and I was also number one in points, and the next year I would have carried #1 but I turned the thing over.

Tom: What happened, did something break on the car or did it just get sideways in slick conditions and get upside down?

Bob: Chuck Spurgin told me before I took off, "Bob, it's getting soft out there, it's starting to get muddy." I said, "Don't worry Charlie, if it starts goin' sideways, I'll shut it off." The next thing I knew the front axle was up at 45 degrees, it just got away from me and flipped. All it did was flip once onto its back, of course we didn't have any safety equipment in those days, no crash helmet. It shoved me down in the cockpit and fractured my skull and broke my right arm. I think I put my right arm over my head to protect myself and that shattered my right elbow.

Tom: In the pictures it looks like the car held up pretty well, considering what it went through when it crashed.

Bob: Oh, yeah. The Veck brothers bought it from me, all they had to do was straighten the body out a little to run it.

Tom: After the Veck brothers bought the car, what happened to it?

Bob: They took my engine out of it. I kept the instruments and some things. The front wheels and tires belonged to Ed Adams, I borrowed them and ran 'em all the time I ran the streamliner, so I took 'em off when I sold the car and gave 'em back. Ed was the first president of SCTA, he really got the whole thing going. We used to go down to Clifton's Cafeteria, he'd lend us a conference room if we bought dinner there. All the members of the clubs that formed the SCTA would meet there.

Tom: Do you have any idea of what became of the car?

Bob: No idea. After the Veck brothers bought it they bought an engine from Bill Worth. I don't know who drove it, I think the best they ever got out of it was 124 mph.

The Skipit Special ran for the Pacemakers before WWII. Built as a street car, the good looking finned machine saw regular lakes duty as well.

TOM: After the crash you got out of racing.

BOB: Yeah. I broke my right arm and I was in the hospital with a concussion for five weeks. This is an interesting note, part of our entry fee, whatever it was, a dollar of it went into a hospital fund, a 100 bucks. That $100 paid for my first week in the hospital. I had $350 in the bank, and that paid for the rest. When I got out of the cast after four or five weeks, I had about an inch and a half of movement, I wondered how the hell I was going to make a living, but after carrying my Skil saw around for a while, it was heavy enough to stretch things back out. It didn't keep me from being a pilot in World War II.

TOM: What did you fly?

BOB: I flew B-17s. I was about eight miles away from Pearl Harbor when it was attacked on December 7, 1941. I was working on some apartments over there. After the

Based on a Chevy chassis, powered by a Chevy four-cylinder with an Olds head, this one-man modified was the basis for the later two-man car.

attack they put us on rebuilding stuff on Ford Island. About the middle of '43 I got to thinking if I was going to do something for the war effort, I'd better get going. I went back to the states and took the tests for cadet training, went through it all as a B-17 pilot. They gave us leave, and while I was home VE day happened. When I came off leave, they sent us back for more training and the Japanese surrendered. I never had a shot fired at me.

TOM: You didn't go back to racing after the war, did you?

BOB: I didn't have the desire to, I had to support my parents, and I wasn't going to take a chance of getting killed. But I still liked building things.

TOM: Didn't you build a boat?

BOB: Yeah, I built a 50-foot sailboat. My wife and I were going to sail it around the world. We lived on it for five years down in Ventura, never did get around to sailing around the world.

TOM: You did some pretty remarkable things during your racing career.

BOB: I guess. Chuck Spurgin and I ran the first streamliner on the lakes. SCTA announced a streamliner class, there was no mention of cubic inches, you could run what you wanted, I thought everyone would show up at the lakes with a streamliner. All Chuck and I had was a two man we were gonna run, so I built a canvas tail on our modified so we could have a streamliner. The tail was made from wood strips, we covered it with muslin, then doped to tighten it up and then painted it black. That was the first streamliner to run SCTA. Then the record in 1940 was kind of a big thing at the time.

TOM: How long did the 140 mph record stand?

BOB: It stood for 10 years. Stu Hilborn broke it in 1950. The record I broke was set by Ernie McAfee.

Nose of the one-man modified was made from a Studebaker gas tank. Trim was made from Ford grille pieces scrounged from a wrecking yard. A proud Bob Rufi sits behind the wheel.

THE WES COOPER COLLECTION

Wes Cooper began racing on the dry lakes of Southern California in the mid-'30s and was a fixture there for the next 50-plus years. He was an ardent racer, a real hard-core hot rodder. Over the years he set numerous records and owned many fine cars.

When Wes passed away a few years ago, he was doing what he loved to do; racing at El Mirage, watching yet another record-breaking pass by one of his engines. A fitting end to a long, colorful career, Wes's ashes were spread on the lake bed; distributed by way of a drag chute at the end of his last pass.

Along with racing, another passion of Wes' was collecting Ford four-cylinder speed equipment. He had amassed a number of rare and unusual examples of Ford aftermarket heads, photos of which are presented here. To describe the collection, Tom Medley called on veteran racer, and Wes Cooper's friend, Bruce Johnston.

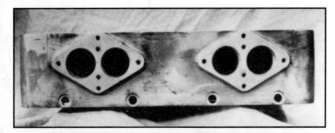

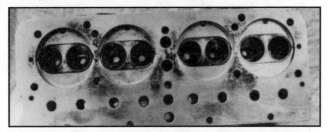

This a late version of a Rutherford head, cast in aluminum, I believe by Don Ferguson. This particular example was machined by Kong Jackson for Wes Cooper. The Rutherford was originally made in cast iron by a fellow named Slim Rutherford, who raced in IMCA and owned and drove a car. Rutherford eventually made his own block, shortly before he retired.

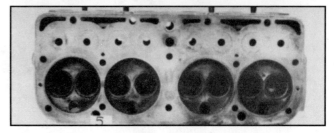

This is a Miller-Schofield, later called a Cragar, probably one of the most popular and common heads ever made for a Model A. It was designed by Leo Goosen, of Miller fame, who also designed all the Miller engines. After one of Millers bankruptcies, a company called Miller-Schofield came to be, and at one time they cranked these heads out. They made quite a few of them.

Photos courtesy of the Wes Cooper estate.

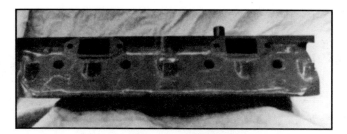
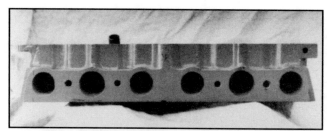

Made in the late '20s and early '30s this is a single overhead cam Howell head for Model A Fords. Built by Harry Hoffsterman in Ohio, Howell heads were never used too much in racing as they didn't perform as well as other designs. There were stories around in the early days that they were made for trucks, I don't know how true that is. You'll notice, this head has intake ports on both sides of the head, which is unusual. You could use the ones on the left or on the right. It was one of the few heads made that way.

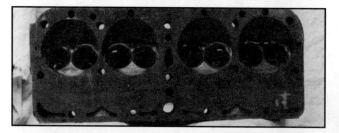

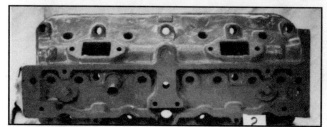

This head is one-of-a-kind. It was built by Art Sparks for a B Class car that ran at Legion Ascot Raceway around 1933. It's a F-head, which means the exhaust valve is in the block and the intake valve is in the head. Art made two heads that were very similar, one was an overhead cam, chain driven, the other was this rocker arm version. You can see by the the combustion chamber this head has one large intake

valve directly over the piston and the exhaust is in the block, similar to a Riley, but a Riley had two intakes.

Another F-head, this one built by Robert Roof of Anderson, Indiana. Roof made stuff back in the days of the T, A and V8-60s. This is similar to the Spark's head, and there were very few of them made. As you can see, it looks like a flat head with rocker arms on top of it. There again it has the intake in the head and the exhaust in the block, it has a much bigger combustion chamber than the Spark's head. This particular head has a pair of very early Winfield carburetors on it with the big intake choke bodies, which acted as silencers. These are barrel valve Winfield's, made very early on, before the S and the SR Winfield carburetors.

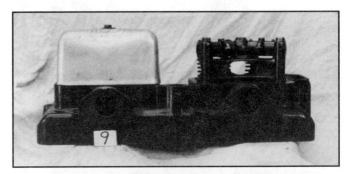

The Riley two-port was probably second in popularity to the Cragar or Miller-Schofield. It came out very early in 1928 and was produced in three versions. Some had the spark plugs on the left, some had the spark plugs on the right, and some had a spark plugs on both sides. This was a very popular head in the early days because it would fit with no alterations. It was inexpensive, and ran real well. Later Riley made a four-port head.

This is a rare head, I'm not real familiar with it, I believe it is called a Rucker. It was built in San Francisco, as the story goes, and there is very little known about it. The head has two intake ports and four exhaust, all on the same side so the standard Model A manifolds would fit. I've only seen two of these heads, so they are not very common.

A Morton-Bret, this head was built in Indianapolis, I assume about the time the Model As came out. It is a two-port intake and a four-port exhaust. However, this one has the intake on the left side, as opposed to the Cragar and others. The rocker arms on this particular head are identical to the SR Fronty, which was also built in Indianapolis. I've always suspected that they used leftover rocker arms from Frontys on these. This head was not very well known on the West Coast, it was more popular in the Midwest.

Another Miller-Schofield, this one happens to have the rocker cover on it. It still has the original writing, and you can see Schofield Incorporated of America. I believe it said: "Must use high test fuel and high compression plugs." Most of these heads in later years had all that writing filed off, so it is rather unusual to find the writing still on one.

This the first of the four-port intake, four-port exhaust heads. The head was originally made about 1934 by the Morales brothers for use at Legion Ascot. It was a single overhead cam in its original form, not a rocker arm. In later years, Joe Gemsa got the pattern from Morales and renamed it the Gemsa head. He converted it to a rocker arm operation, although he did build a few overhead cam versions, too. This was a well-designed head, they ran very good.

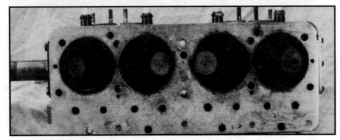

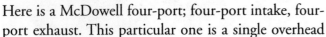

Here is a McDowell four-port; four-port intake, four-port exhaust. This particular one is a single overhead cam version. Ray McDowell built two-port and four-port heads and also double overhead cam heads. In the early days he was located in Hollywood, then he moved to Burbank. The heads were used primarily on oval track race cars, it was a very successful design.

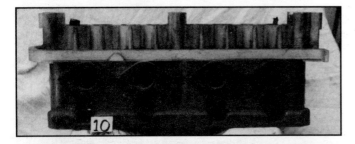

Unfortunately there is only one picture of a Pop Evans turbulence A-Head. Pop Evans was an early day race driver, and became quite well known in California as the maintenance man who prepared all the tracks. He would run his old Model A race car around the tracks, stopping now and then to patch the track. Then he'd run a few more laps. The first time I saw him he appeared to be an old man, and he didn't look any different 20 or 30 years later. The guys in the early days of racing would talk about going to Flagstaff to race. Pop had an early version of a house trailer, which was unknown then, and would tow it to Flagstaff with his race car. He was quite a character, big handlebar mustache, a very friendly man.

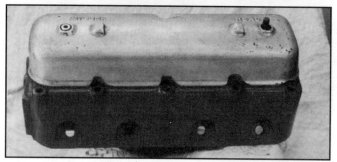

A very rare piece, this is an early Miller-Schofield. All that can be seen on the rocker cover is Miller Head, the rest has been ground off. This particular model is what is called the slope side. The left side of the head is not vertical as it was on the later heads made by Cragar. Why they changed it is unknown, because the sloped heads didn't crack, and all the later ones did. There were very few of these slant-sided Millers built.

Another Miller-Schofield head with the writing ground off. As opposed to the previous head, the left side of this one is square, not sloping. This is the way most were made by Miller-Schofield, and later by Cragar. These heads were very popular, and probably more of them were built than any other Model A head. Unfortunately, almost every one of them cracked at the center head bolt, between the number two and three spark plugs, and they had to be welded.

Built by George White, of Bell Auto Parts, was the Cragar Junior. It was designed to go in a small Continental block, it was very similar to the improved Cragar for the Model A. This particular one was designed for midget race cars and has Riley side draft carburetors on it that George Riley made just after WWII. The carburetors were more successful than the head.

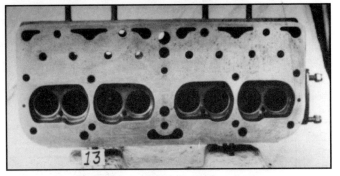

This is the last version of the Cragar, it was the so-called improved Cragar. The intake ports are on the left instead of between the exhaust ports on the right, as on the early ones. In this picture you can see Bell Auto Parts written on the rocker cover. This head was made by George White, who owned Bell Auto Parts, after the Cragar company ceased to exist. There was much debate about the improved design, many felt the combustion chamber was shrouded too much.

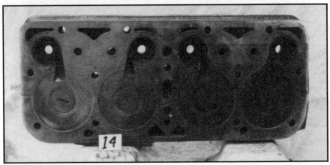

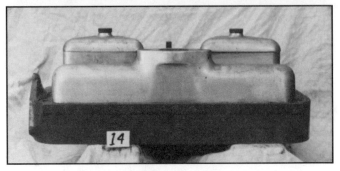

A one-of-a-kind Diesel conversion head for a Model A. Can you imagine a Model A living with the compression that this head created? There is practically no combustion chamber. It had the overhead intake on the left side, and the exhaust was in the block. It was another F-head conversion. This was the only one I have ever seen.

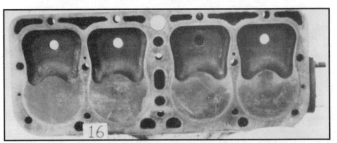

This is the Winfield flat head for the Model A. There were thousands of these made. There were two versions: the yellow head and the red head. The only difference was the compression ratio. The yellow head was 6:1 and I believe the other was 7:1. Looking at the chamber of this one it appears to be one of the higher compression red heads.

A head I'm not really familiar with is this Simons Super Power Head. It says on it "For Model A Fords—Licensed by Chrysler Motors" this head is a mystery to me. The combustion chamber is unusual because the fuel was so bad in those days, everyone was searching for a design that would stop detonation.

 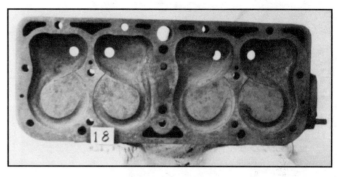

Another example of the combustion chamber design search to stop detonation. I don't know who made this one, it is a High Turbulence head with a patent pending. The spark plug recesses are notched so water will run out when it rains and won't short the spark plug. Very unusual head.

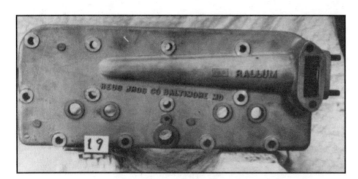 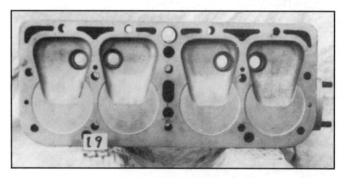

Another one of the many flatheads made for Model As. This says Roose Bros, Baltimore, Maryland. Something interesting on this one is the name cast in the water outlet: "Rallum." It might have been a play on Harry Miller and one of his bankruptcies when he spelled his name backwards: Rellim.

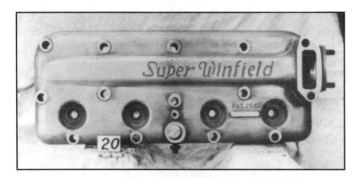 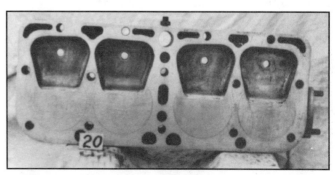

This is a later version of the Winfield; I think they were made with reworked patterns from the early ones. The later heads say Super Winfield, but the Super script is slightly different than the Winfield. Also this head was made out of aluminum and it used 14 mm spark plugs, instead of the larger 18 mm as with the older heads.

Another of the many flathead designs. This head has an odd combustion chamber shape and spark plug location. This head does not have any provisions for a Model A water pump, although the head is for a Model A and not for a T, as I first thought. The name, Coisson, I'm not familiar with.

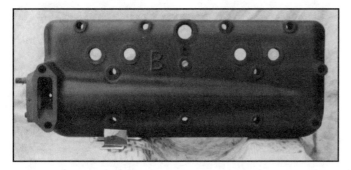
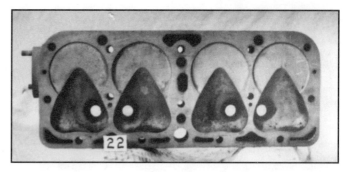

This is a Ford production head with a B cast on top, although it was not for the Model B, the Model B head had a C cast on top. This was supposedly a high performance head for a Model A or B, and to the best of my knowledge was manufactured by Ford.

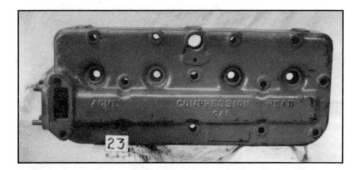

Another version of a flathead, the Acme. It looks like something may have been ground off of it, as there is a large space between Acme and Compression. One of many designs, notice the spark plug location. This head has the plugs over towards the edge of the piston. I don't know how successful this design was.

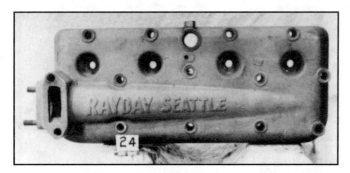

This head says RAY DAY, Seattle. I assume it was the same company that made Ray Day pistons, which were far more well known than the Ray Day flathead. Here again, a conventional chamber with not very high compression.

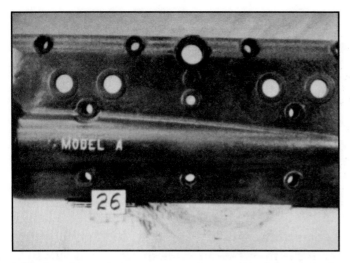 

This head is unknown to me. It says Model A, which could mean most anything. I don't believe it was built by Ford. The spark plugs are toward the intake valve, which according to today's technology is the wrong place. I don't know who made this head, it is the only one I have ever seen.

In addition to the heads shown in these pictures, there were several double overhead cam heads built for the Model A and B, primarily for the oval track. Dreyer built one in Indianapolis that was very successful. He later made his own block because he couldn't keep the Ford together.

Hal over in Ohio made a DOHC head for a Model A, and later made a five main block of his own.

Ray McDowell, in Burbank, made a double overhead cam head. The first version was a 16-valve design, but he had trouble with them cracking, so he switched to an eight-valve version. There wasn't much known about air flow in those days.

Probably the nicest built and the best of them all was the Leo Goosen design from Harry Miller. The first half-dozen were known as Miller-Fords, and were one of the most successful two-cam head designs made for Fords.

Another four-cylinder that isn't mentioned here was basically a Chevrolet design made by John Gerber, in Iowa. He started out racing with four-cylinder Chevy's but couldn't keep them together. So, he finally made a head and block that looked almost identical to the Chevy, but it had five mains and a single overhead cam. It was a two-port intake, three-port exhaust, like the Olds head that was commonly used on the four-cylinder Chevy. This thing was near unbeatable for many years through the Midwest.

Another successful head was the Winfield rocker arm design. There were only five or six made, about 1934, when Legion Ascot lowered the compression ratio limit to 7:1 and the displacement limit to 200 cubic inches. This head was designed by Ed Winfield, and used on a car driven by Rex Mays. It was very, very successful, especially on the shorter tracks; it was probably the fastest rocker arm head around. It was four-port intake, four-port exhaust. I worked on it in later years, and the reason it was so successful was not the head design, but the camshaft. On his own engines Ed had cam grinds that were comparable to today's design, as far as lift and duration; however he wouldn't sell them to anybody else.

About the same time, Winfield built a flathead for Willy Utzman that ran just about as good as the rocker arm equipped engines. This thing had 330 degrees of valve duration, unheard of in 1934, and enormous ports. It was driven by the real hot dogs of the time, and sat on the front row of the mile at El Centro against the Millers. At the Oakland mile it sat on the front row against 11 Millers. It didn't stay together as well as the Millers, but it did run.

Ed Winfield knew in those days to put a lot of camshaft and a lot of rpm in his motors. I know for a fact, because I owned, and drove the car in later years; they were turning that flathead 6,500 rpm, and I was told it would hit 7,000 on some occasions. Ed was smart enough to know that high rpm and a low gear would win coming out of the corners. He also knew that it took a lot of cam to get that rpm, and he wouldn't grind one for anybody else.

STREET RODS MAKE A COMEBACK

While drag racing and car shows were taking their own directions in hot rodding, and many hot rodders of the '40s and '50s were drifting over to serious circle track and sports car competitions, there remained a very devoted group of people who enjoyed the more traditional type of hot rod. This was the daily driven vehicle, in either hot rod or custom design, which has rightfully been called America's true sports car.

As drag racing began to specialize in the late 1950s, dual-purpose street/strip cars were no longer competitive. At the same time, high-performance vehicles from Detroit made the '30s- and '40s-style hot rods obsolete, in handling as well as in horsepower. By 1957, there were only a handful of old-style rods and customs on the streets of Southern California, and the situation was not much better across the country. Magazines continued to show the traditional rod and custom cars, but more and more these vehicles were made for the show circuit.

If there is one single event responsible for the rebirth of traditional-type hot rods, it would be the formation of the Los Angeles

When the Los Angeles Roadster Club organized in 1957, there was almost no traditional hot rod activity in Southern California. Small cruises on weekends led to larger and larger gatherings, the beginnings of modern rod runs.

When street rodding began a comeback in the 1960s, a few of the older cars were returned to road use, such as the Highland Plating Special track T. Here one sports a fenderless Mullins camping trailer, starting a continuing trend for tagalongs.

Custom cars of the '30s through the early '50s were generally built more for appearance than performance, but there were a few cross-over customs that ran hard at the lakes and drags. This '36 Ford roadster used a Packard grille and Buick headlight buckets.

Street rods were the backbone of hot rodding up into the early 1950s, rod club activities included plenty of open road driving such as the Pasadena Roadster Club reliability runs. This spirit of driving the hot rod still permeates the hobby.

Roadster Club. Dick Scritchfield, veteran of the salt flats and drags, had purchased a very nice 1932 fenderless Ford roadster. Noting the lack of old-time rods on the road, he began contacting other roadster owners to see if there was any interest in forming a club. The first official meeting was held on a lawn just down the street from Phil Weiand's manufacturing plant. The publisher of this book, Tex Smith, was in attendance, and he remembers that the half dozen or so founding members voiced a common desire... to promote interest in the traditional hot rod. To everyone present, that meant roadster.

In the years to come, several Roadster Club members would form or join new clubs that were open to closed cars, but the idea for most of these organizations was the preservation of a disappearing piece of American history.

Members of the L.A. Roadsters were active at the dry lakes and the drags. Most were attending shows, but all wanted to do open road activities. Such events were not unknown, since hot rod clubs of the '30s and '40s had sponsored reliability runs and tours, and clubs of the

The emphasis of hot rodding in earlier times was on driving a high performance car. Removing the fenders in good climate areas such as Southern California was a natural continuation of the Model T "strip down" philosophy.

This full-fendered '29A-V8 is a timeless roadster design.

Gene Cross of Iowa was at the first street rod nationals, he shares some snapshots of the event. Here is a rest stop en route; in 1970 the theme was "getting there is half the fun."

The first rod nationals show segment was held on a freshly mowed hay field. Street rods had evolved considerably from those of the late '40s.

Jim Babbs built a miniature C-Cab rod, using a Subaru engine. The car was so small and nimble that it dominated the other rods in Streetkhana at the initial nationals.

'50s were heavily into poker runs (but with a preponderance of late model cars). The L.A. Roadster Club started with cruises to points of interest in the Los Angeles basin, usually including a picnic. Members worked up new types of driving events, such as Highway Bingo, and many of the club events were covered by *HOT ROD MAGAZINE*. The weekend cruises became longer, and soon a Northern California roadster club debuted. It was obvious that a meeting of the Los Angeles and the Bay Area Roadster Clubs was in order. This Roadster Roundup was the catalyst to convince other groups around the country, and Canada, that street rodding was alive and well.

From this meager beginning in 1957, the traditional form of hot rodding began a slow climb from oblivion, thanks in very large measure to the specialty clubs such as the L.A. and Bay Area Roadsters, and the Early Times (a closed car club). In other areas, traditional clubs were reemerging, or forming, with an emphasis on street-driven vehicles. All of this was immediately apparent to the staff of *ROD & CUSTOM MAGAZINE*.

In the mid-1960s, I had moved from *HOT ROD* to *ROD & CUSTOM*, which had Bud Bryan, Dick Scritchfield, John Christy and Jim Jacobs on staff, and Tex

Smith as a freelance contributor. Knowing what was happening in the car hobby, we decided to slant the magazine format toward street rodding and traditional customs. There was a huge need for information, but there was essentially no street rod industry to supply parts.

Street rodding was happening everywhere, with events of local and regional character. Tex and I had casually discussed the idea of a national street rod run for a couple of years before the entire crew sat down in my office to plan such an event. The idea was to bring as many street rods as possible together in one place, the object being to see how many street rods were actually on the road, and to present a unified front of rodders to impress state lawmakers. Driving a traditional type of hot rod was still a problem in the '60s. At that time, we also discussed how inclusive our invitation should be. It was decided that the acceptable model year cut-off would be through 1948, since that was the general end of clamshell fenders. This would restrict the "decal" cars from attendance, late models that were high performance but hardly what we had in mind as traditional hot rods.

We felt that the event should be held in the approximate population center of the

This chopped '34 sedan, which was driven from California, featured a supercharged engine. A magazine feature car, it created quite a stir among Midwestern rodders.

The first rod nationals was an initial chance for many rod builders to compare talents with West Coast rodders. This channeled '27 T roadster took a back seat to none.

Sam Gregory had his Chevy sedan at the first nationals. Sam went on to build the Chevy into a bombshell during the '80s.

Events at the early street rod nationals, and at local events as well, were more for the delight of spectators than of rodders. Still, those rodders who took part, as in this greased pig chase, considered doing things more important than sitting in lawn chairs.

United States in order to have a good turnout. We knew a large run had been attempted in the Madison, Wisconsin, area, and we knew that we needed a volunteer club to make the thing work. About then, Bruce Miller from Peoria, Illinois, contacted us and said that he and the local Slo-Pokes club would be glad to work as hosts. The Minnesota Street Rod Association added their support, so we were off and running.

Miller contacted the Peoria Chamber of Commerce, the mayor, and other city officials. I exchanged letters with the mayor explaining what we had in mind. It was

Although Fat Fords would gain widespread popularity in the mid-'80s, this sedan delivery from Iowa was ahead of its time at Memphis.

Contrary to legend, there were plenty of closed hot rods in the Southern California area during earlier years, as this 1934 five-window coupe shows.

full speed ahead. A proposal for the event, to be sponsored by *ROD & CUSTOM MAGAZINE*, was presented to our Petersen Publishing Company 7th floor decision makers, without receiving much encouragement. That didn't dull our enthusiasm, so we announced the event in the August 1970 issue of *R&C*. We also ran stories on the laws of different states regarding hot rods traveling through, and a street rod nats last-minute bulletin was published just before the event.

At the same time, the National Street Rod Association was being formed. Earlier, Tex had consulted with the National Hot Rod Association about forming a division for street-oriented cars, but the NHRA had declined because it had so much to do just with drag racing. Bruce Miller had suggested a national street association, so it was left to him to follow through. Bruce formed the NSRA, with Cotton Werksman of Barrington, Illinois. Cotton incorporated NSRA in the state of Illinois, and he ran it (along with his wife) for a couple of years. Dues were $5 per year. I designed the logo for letterheads, etc., and coined the phrase: "Street is Neat."

Although roadster clubs got the rod run thing going again, the closed cars soon joined the fun. Now they outnumber open cars handily.

Mo Greenlee didn't need a hood covering the huge blower in his 1940 Ford coupe.

Another California car, this T touring packed plenty of travel gear on the running boards and the accessory trunk.

To raise money for this initial nationals, freelancer Tex Smith would cash his *R&C* checks (which were never very big) and send the money back to me for the Nationals Fund. Although the official title was the *ROD & CUSTOM* Street Rod Nationals, there was no actual support from PPC. The money we had for the event with was extremely limited, but we made do. We were off for Peoria, wondering how many cars would show up, what the weather

A major reason that turnkey rod builders became a part of street rodding was the effort of builder Andy Brizio of the San Francisco Bay Area. This C-Cab was a product of his shop, and it was driven as part of a caravan from Northern California to Tennessee.

Street rods of the late '40s and early '50s were quality rides in areas where hot rodding had been around for a long time.

Orv Elgie from Southern California built a '37 Ford sedan delivery in the '60s, and drove it to Illinois for the nationals.

would be, and if the event would be a success.

We were headquartered at the Sands Motel (since torn down), a modest downtown place with a modest parking lot adjacent. We had gathered material from various hot rod suppliers, and we had some special imprinted shopping bags from a major hot rod tire company. These were the first "Goodie Bags." The day prior to official event opening, our staff was considering exactly what we should do. We felt that a registration of some sort would be in order, and Tex's wife Pegge volunteered to set one up in the motel parking lot. She had experience with that from NHRA. Her crew were wives and girlfriends of the street rodders.

We had no idea how many cars would show up. We had pre-registration of nearly 300 rods and customs, which we considered a huge number. As it turned out, nearly 100 of these did not show up, mostly because the cars were unfinished. But when we looked out the motel window on the morning of opening day, we were amazed: The motel parking lot and the adjacent parking lot were crammed with cars. They were everywhere! There were over 600 cars at that first nationals, from nearly every state and Canada.

This simulated chain-drive speedster was knee high, and it received a huge amount of attention at the first nationals.

Registration ran smoothly, mostly because we had no idea what a street rod registration should be. But we were mostly winging it for activity. Early Saturday morning we figured we needed something for the unexpectedly large turnout to do. Tex said he could put together a Streetkhana in about 30 minutes if a place could be found. One of the Slo-Pokes made a phone call and a nearby theater parking lot was commandeered, along with some traffic cones. Word of mouth filled the theater parking lot with spec-

Getting out and getting under became a ritual with street rodders heading cross country to major events.

Entertainment at the Memphis nationals was presented on an outdoor stage. Rodders enjoyed these big event extras.

tators and participants. The eventual winner of this initial national driving event was radiator guru Jim Babbs and his Subaru-powered C-Cab called "itty-bits."

We had planned ahead for a special Show 'n' Shine, to take place at the Timberline Farms campgrounds, 22 miles east of Peoria. The owner of the campgrounds, Mr. Foster, was a very supportive host, even mowing a hay field to accommodate the extra cars. The response by everyone was mostly disbelief! Over 600 street rods and customs were in one place.

The awards presentation and participant barbeque were held at the farm, out in the open. As soon as

This supercharged small block Chevy V8 in a Model A coupe is not too far distant from the As of the '40s, yet it was possible to add independent suspension, air conditioning, power steering, and many comfort options not available to earlier rodders.

The turtle race at the second hot rod nationals had a strong entry field.

Merchandise giveaways started with the first rod nationals, and escalated to the giveaway of a complete engine at Memphis.

everyone had eaten, the awards were presented from a makeshift stage: an old farm wagon. The P.A. system was powered by the world's longest extension cord. It was all crude, but no one cared. This was FUN!!! That first street rod nationals awards presentation was a major race against time… and gathering storm clouds. When Emcee Tex Smith asked if everyone would like to have another Nationals, the resounding "YES!" was thunderous. And then a major league Midwest storm turned the area into a sea of mud. Thus ended the very first Street Rod Nationals.

From that beginning, organized national street rodding was underway. NSRA didn't grow quickly, but it grew steadily. Each successive nationals was larger than the last until the magic (and unthinkable) number of 10,000 participants was met. Local and regional street rod and custom runs have emerged, some

The beginnings of the RestoRod theme in street rodding appeared at Memphis nationals. This 1932 Chevy coupe is a great example of the rodded restoration.

The Show 'n' Shine became a major part of every rod run, starting the trend toward rod runs as huge outdoor car shows.

One of the major attractions of rod runs to street rodders is the emphasis on family, unlike racing.

drawing over 6,000 participants. Street rodding has erupted in many foreign countries, as well, easily supporting its claim as the world's biggest participant automotive group. The sport has a strong manufacturing and sales industry, and by all counts it is going to continue. A very fitting tribute to those intrepid hot rodders who first ventured onto Southern California dry lakes all those many decades ago.

In 1971 the street rod nationals moved to the fairgrounds in Memphis, Tennessee. The number of participants was up from Peoria, but still not a portent of the 10,000-plus entrants that were to eventually make street rodding the most visible part of hot rodding.

Street rodding has brought out lots of cars that had never seriously been considered rodding material before. This MoPar coupe is a prime example.

Dick and Lois Megugorac drove this 327-cubic-inch Chevy-powered '27 T touring from Los Angeles to Memphis. Magoo would gain fame as the operator of a turnkey street rod shop.

Street rodding was given a big boost in the late '50s when Cal Automotive introduced their fiberglass T body, then Norm Grabowski caught rodders' fancies with his Kookie T of TV fame. This led to a continuing line of "Fad T's," such as these examples at Memphis.

100 MPH JALLOPIES RACE ON THE DESERT

BY HENRY F. UNGER

Streaking through the hot, alkali dust of Muroc Dry Lake, in the Mohave Desert, a tiny, buglike racing car snapped a wire stretched across its course. A quarter mile farther on, it hurtled into another wire. When judges consulted the electric timing apparatus, they announced that E. C. McAfee, piloting the diminutive speedster, had hit a speed of 127.60 miles an hour—setting a new record for the tin-can racers that compete in the strange and thrilling amateur speed meets held by the Southern California Timing Association.

Three weeks before, McAfee's car had been only a mass of tubing and the block of an untried four-cylinder stock motor sitting on a garage floor. Hours of spare-time work had transformed it into a streamline racer which now carried off highest honors in a hotly contested tournament of thrills.

But young McAfee was not satisfied. Before the next race day arrived, he applied the shears and cut another hole through the cowling to cool the engine some more. Then on the cracked surface of Harper's Dry Lake, he pointed the rounded nose of his homemade car down the straightaway. The starter's red flag dropped; wheels bit into the bone-dry earth, and electrical timing devices recorded the almost incredible speed of 132 miles an hour as the home-built jallopy skimmed through the measured quarter mile.

E. C. McAfee in the tin-can racing car with which he set a record of 132 miles an hour. He built it in only three weeks.

There isn't room in the tiny cockpit for a wheel, so two handles are attached to the post for steering.

Although it isn't much for looks, this four-cylinder Model B Ford, with a special valve-and-head job, made 100.96 miles an hour.

This is a reprint of an article which first appeared in the February, 1939 edition of POPULAR SCIENCE MAGAZINE.

McAfee's car, on whose side blazes the number "1" as testimony that he has qualified at a higher speed than any other of the 200 members of the association, was built of stainless-steel tubes and thin sheets of metal. Some of the fleet little cars that compete in these amateur race meets are beautiful creations of master garage craftsmen, but most of them are small roadsters and modified coupes, fitted with a variety of devices intended to push the cars above the 100-mile-an-hour mark.

These speed dashes, held on dry lakes of the Mohave Desert in Southern California, have no counterpart anywhere in the world. No money purses lure the contestants. Free regrinding jobs and coveralls, awarded by supply firms are the only prizes they can expect for setting new records or for winning mile-long races down a flag-marked straightaway. Yet no driver at the classic Indianapolis sweepstakes ever strove harder to win than do these mechanics and service-station workers who "hit the desert" four times each year to drive through scorching heat and blinding dust in quest of new records.

It's all very official and accurate, too. Twenty-eight clubs form the association. Between dusk and midnight of a Saturday night, each club will rendezvous somewhere near Los Angeles. Night Flyers meet outside Pasadena; the Gophers on another side road; Mercuries, Sidewinders, Comets, 90-Mile-An-Hour entries, Idlers, and Road Runners form their own parties. Some of the racers are driven; others are towed and a few ride on trucks. Through the night these strange caravans move along the highway through San Bernardino, Victorville, Barstow, and on to Muroc or Harper Dry Lake.

Through early morning hours, the technical committee labors to install the electrical timing system. A quarter mile apart to the inch, two wires stretch across the course, each leading to a recording disk at the judges' stand, which consists simply of an overturned airplane motor crate and an umbrella. At dawn, the first driver to arrive on the starting line gets the "Go!" signal. He may drift past the starter at forty miles an hour, or leap forward from a standing start, helped by five or six bystanders eager to see each car turn its maximum speed. One mile away, he enters the trap,

An official whites a speedometer face so the driver will not hold back to qualify for a slower rating.

A racer speeding through the trap in a qualifying run.

Entries lined up at sunrise for the qualifying trial runs. The speed registered by a car in this test determines the class in which it will compete during the afternoon races.

emerging as he flashes past the alert judges.

On his return, a judge marks his speed on a small card attached to the left door of the car. Between sunup and noon, more than 400 trials will be run, one contestant moving down the straightaway as his predecessor disappears in a dust cloud down the narrow lane. Like jack rabbits, these boys jump toward the finish line. Each is expected to drive at top speed, to qualify for races which take place during the afternoon. To make sure that none eases up on the throttle to qualify for a slower class, an official smears whiting over the faces of the speedometer and the tachometer, the instrument that shows motor speed.

As I stood beside the judges' stand recently observing the trials, I noted that few failed to pass the 100-mile-an-hour mark. Disappointment was registered on alkali-crusted faces behind wheels which had steered occasional cars through somewhere in the nineties. Back went those drivers for another try.

This snappy car was constructed by Dave West, Culver City garage man.

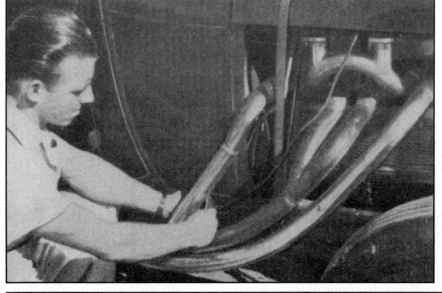

Long exhaust pipes rigged along the sides of some cars, as at the left, reduce the danger of fires being started by hot gas.

You hear strange arguments about the respective merits of flatheads, Crager heads, three-port heads, Winfield heads, V-8 heads, Tornado heads, McDowell heads, four-port heads. Each driver expresses his own preference. You find Ford Model B four-cylinder and V-8 motors, Chevrolets, Buicks, a Pierce Arrow, Terraplanes. Anything goes, with two exceptions. Drivers must race American production engines, and cannot use double overhead cam jobs.

Walk down the long line of cars awaiting their turns at the starting line, and you see twin carburetors projecting through the cowling of one car; a single, long exhaust pipe on another; four individual exhausts curving from a third; open

The judges' stand is just an overturned airplane-motor crate with a rough desk and stools set on it.

It was considered quite an achievement to coax 86.43 miles an hour out of this four-cylinder Chevrolet of 1927 vintage.

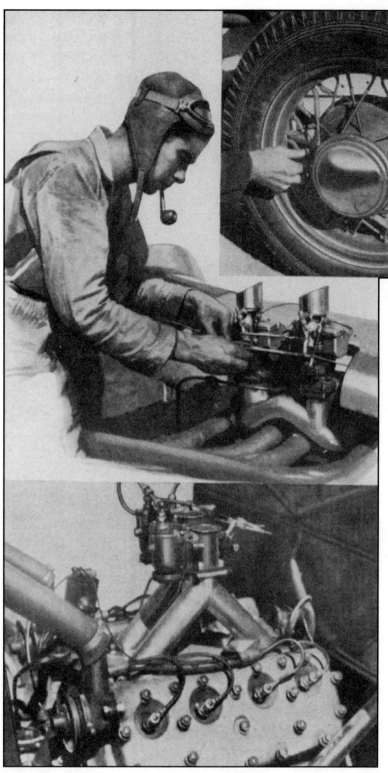

Staggered, inverted V-shaped manifolds distribute gas to the eight cylinders of this engine. Above, a driver adjusting his dual carburetors whose intakes protrude through the car's hood.

water. Many ingenious methods and devices, all pointed toward greater speed.

Too, you hear will-nigh unbelievable tales of achievement; then you see those same incredible cars leap down the lake, and from the timers you hear of another record falling. Dave West, a Culver City mechanic in No. 94, which means that ninety-three other cars are faster than his, fixes 100 miles an hour as his goal, and triumphantly demands that you "set down 113," a few minutes later, on returning from his first trial spin. Official, too, Karl Orr spent $900 on his four-cylinder motor, tinkering and improving. He was rewarded with 115 miles an hour. But W. C. Warth, with a much smaller investment, perhaps $400, now jams the throttle down for 129.41 miles an hour.

Spider Smalley, one of the Pasadena Night Flyers, clocked 111 in a Ford roadster. Spider installed a 1932 Model B Ford motor in a 1929 chassis. He bought overhead valves, a large carburetor and manifold, and reground the cams—"There's the secret," he whispers. He installed racing bearings and high-duty, high-dome aluminum-alloy pistons and changed to 3.27-1 gearings. And, as a result, he had a mechanical jack rabbit capable of wind-splitting speed.

Glenn Stone and Brooks Walling of the Hot Iron club at Canoga Park put together a '29 roadster chassis and a '32 engine block. Except for pistons and a new truck crankshaft, these boys picked up discarded parts. They pushed their jallopy up to 108.43 miles an hour. Bob Cressey and Al Brush owned a motor and chassis, respectively. They combined the best features of both, and rang up 101 before modifying the body for increased speed.

"There's the real secret of the fascination of this strange sport—unlimited enthusiasm and decidedly

roadsters and roadsters covered with canvas, with drivers' crash-helmeted heads projecting through small holes—this for streamlining; twin, staggered manifolds; lead coils on spokes to balance wheels, helpers filling radiators from vacuum jugs of chilled

limited pocketbooks. Money and time are spent with no hope for material rewards. On the side lines you hear the boys arguing about power outputs, reduced cam action, tachometer readings. One motor winds up 6,300 r.p.m., another 5,800, yet the slower engine produces a winner. You can be sure that new gears and faster-acting cams will spell a different result at the next meeting of the association.

Meetings are held on Sundays during the summer only, because winter weather leaves the old lake beds in a soggy condition. Owing to the shortness of the run, most drivers remove their fan belts, thereby disconnecting water pumps and generators. All unnecessary trimmings, such as fenders, bumpers, windshields, and spare tires are eliminated, to lighten the cars and enable them to turn up maximum speed. In a phaeton, the back seat is covered with a tonneau shield, usually of canvas, to give a streamline effect and prevent eddies of air that would hold the racer back.

At early meetings, coupes and sedans appeared among the entries, but it was soon found that these could not keep pace with open cars. Although a few of the more fortunate drivers are equipped with crash helmets, the majority of them content themselves with leather headgear and goggles.

Afternoon races provide an exciting climax to the trials, but these form a less important part of the lake runs. Three and four abreast, the little cars roar through the dust. Occasionally, one smashes into the crowd. It was Smalley, blinded by dust, whose ignition cut out while following the leaders at a clip passing the hundred mark. "She blew up," he tells you. "What's a guy to do? Spin her! At seventy, I slithered between two parked cars while hot water poured back through the fire wall." But that doesn't happen very often. Just frequently enough to bring crowds of 15,000 to some of the trials, which are held secretly in order to discourage even larger gatherings at these nerve-tingling race meets behind the hills fringing the Mohave Desert.

Latest in streamlining—a driver's head, topped with a crash helmet, sticks up through a canvas sheathing.

On the hot, dry desert, racers fill their radiators with ice water from large vacuum jugs.

TOM'S SCRAPBOOK

The amazing thing about doing a history book, any kind of history it would seem, is that you always end up with reams of material that simply doesn't seem to fit any specific niche. It may be a single paragraph of text, or an entire chapter. One small photo or drawing, or an entire folio. And, most generally, it is all just too important to leave out of print. Such is the case here.

In our initial Tom Medley Hot Rod History, Book One, we didn't have enough room to include the tremendous material on Wes Cooper's great Model A Ford head collection. Nor did we have room to include some early event programs. This time, they were the first things we scheduled. Even so, as material began to accumulate at Medley's Southern California home, it became readily evident we would need a very special section in this

MISC. STUFF FROM THE SALT AND THE LAKES
(with a couple other things thrown in just to keep you on your toes)

Bob Higbee, SCTA Bonneville starter, gets ready to turn AK Miller loose on one of his flat-out trips through the lights en route to the D Class modified roadster first place trophy.

AK Miller's 1953 Bonneville entry was this 320-cubic-inch Olds V8-powered D Class modified roadster. AK walked away with the top speed of the week of 174.08 mph.

A D Lakester belly tank gets a push start down the course during the '53 Bonneville Nationals. Top speed in this class was 212.51 mph, posted by the Breene-Haller Chrysler V8 entry.

second book. And it would be, of necessity, a kind of potpourri of hot rodding. A scrapbook type of thing where we could tuck and squeeze and fit in all the pieces that simply didn't go in better defined chapters.

We won't include another biography on author Tom Medley, we did that rather extensively in Book One. Still, we should remind our readers that Medley was involved in hot rodding in the Oregon area well before World War II, that he is to this day an excellent jitterbug dancer, that he was an original member of the *HOT ROD MAGAZINE* staff (retiring only recently from Petersen Publishing Company), and that he has been there/seen that/done that in just about every facet of the automotive performance scene.

Currently he tools around the nation in one of the sweetest Chevy-powered 1940 Ford coupes to be found, the tape deck belting out tunes from

Tommy Dorsey, Glen Miller, Artie Shaw... well, you get the idea.

Thus, we present the Tom Medley Scrapbook. Some of the photos Tom has information on, many more are just things that were in the file cabinet. They may be of very important people before they were VIP. Or they may be photos of interesting equipment that never made the cover of *THROTTLE* magazine, or the decade-later *HOT ROD*. If you wonder why so many photos from Bonneville and the dry lakes, remember that those were the places where rod builders could go to check the performance of their ideas. In those days, a favorite saying was, "If it don't go, chrome it!" Meaning show cars normally weren't serious race cars. Ordinary daily driven hot rods were much less photographed than race cars, probably because they were so common. But all of this is history... Hot Rod History. If you're reading this book, you will surely agree that nothing needs to be shared more.

A typical early morning starting line scene at El Mirage, 1947 SCTA meet. The roadster with its hood off belongs to Harvey Haller, the B Class roadster ran 128.57 mph at this meet.

A great look down the course in 1953, looks like you could go forever—not so today!

Third fastest B Modified roadster at '53 Bonneville Nationals was the Nero Evans "Salt Shaker" with a speed of 150.25. Power was supplied by a 259-inch Merc flat motor. Owner belonged to the SCTA Dolphins Club.

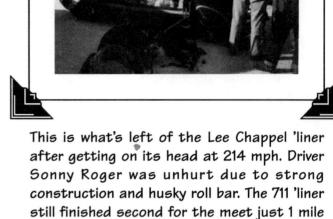

The Lee Chappel C Streamliner was on hand for the '53 Bonneville get together. Powered by a V8 engine equipped with Tornado OHV heads, this sleek 'liner ran 230.62 for the second fastest time in the class.

This is what's left of the Lee Chappel 'liner after getting on its head at 214 mph. Driver Sonny Roger was unhurt due to strong construction and husky roll bar. The 711 'liner still finished second for the meet just 1 mile an hour slower than the Shadoff Special streamliner.

The C Class roadster entry of Barlow Hadley captured the class fast time of the week with a speed of 165.13 mph and a first place trophy. Power was generated by a 300-inch Chrysler V8.

The Don Waite-Bradshaw B Modified roadster gets a push start at the salt. This "Edelbrock Special," running a 257-cubic-inch DeSoto V8 placed first in its class.

LeRoy Neumayer drove the Casel-Fugatt C Class modified roadster to a top speed of 190.57, capturing first place in the C modified roadster class. Power was by a 284-inch Merc.

Jim Culbert, San Diego speed merchant, awaits the start at Bonneville Nationals. His C Modified rear-engined roadster turned in the fourth fastest C Class speed of 173.07 mph. A 296-cubic-inch Merc engine supplied the horses.

Home-built streamliner from Denver, Colorado, powered by a Olds V8 engine, its best time was 142.40 mph. Driven by A.R. Thompson.

Bill Waddill from Flint, Michigan, came all the way to the salt to turn 143.76 mph in his modified sedan. Good looking car.

The crew hard at work on the Chet Herbert D Class streamliner. Driven by LeRoy Neumayer, this slippery creation took top honors at the '53 salt fest with a speed of 211.39 mph. Muscle by a 356-cube Chrysler V8. This car also set the fastest time of the International Record Trials September 8-11 with a one-way speed of 246 mph.

Top time in the D Lakester Class was posted by the Haller & Breene entry during the '53 salt shootout. This small size aircraft wing tank was stuffed with a 364 Chrysler Hemi V8. As can be seen in the photo, the rear tire has lost tread on one of the over-200 mph runs. Winning time for the meet was 212.51 mph with Harvey Haller at the wheel.

Mickey Thompson's dual-engined E Competition coupe. One Chrysler Hemi V8 and a Merc flathead supplied the power. A total of 600 cubic inches for a top speed of 164.53 mph.

The Shadoff Chrysler Special was top dog in the C streamliner competition at the '53 salt meet, blasting a time of 231.66 mph. Later the following month, September, it was the first car to capture an International Record, streaking through the traps at 236 mph. Hal Hooper was the driver, Carl Fleishmann built the car, and Ray Brown built the engine, a 300-cubic-inch Hemi Chrysler. A dynamite combination.

The C modified roadster entry from Dahm Brothers-Hurst awaits the start. Best time of 153.84 came from a 304-inch Merc flat motor.

Dick Kraft lights off his bob tailed roadster at an early SCTA Lakes meet on El Mirage.

It's front blower repair right out on the salt. Gotta get it right for the next run!

Tommie Lee's Offie-powered streamliner. Ran 130 mph in the late '40s.

A blown 259 Merc flathead V8 powered the Fox and Cobb / So-Cal Speed Shop entry to a two-way average of 172 mph and the C Competition coupe gold.

An X-Ray view of the C&T Automotive very successful oval track roadster powered by a Ardun-equipped Ford V8 engine. A very strong runner.

A Russetta Timing Association '34 coupe from the Hutter's of Whittier, California, heads down the long flat salt.

A chopped '34 tudor with early '50s graphics gets a push start down the long black line of the Bonneville salt.

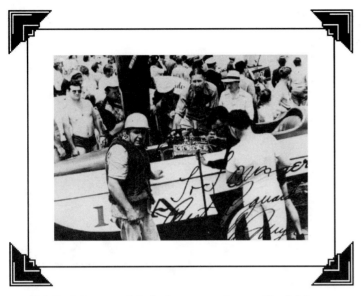

Eddie Meyer, with helmet, and son Bud Meyer work on their V8 powered inboard racing boat.

Wild full-fendered channeled '34 five window Ford coupe. Check the shortened grille and headlight position.

A very sharp '29 on '32 rails street roadster. This neat little car was on the LA streets in 1947.

The So-Cal Speed Shop A Class tank proceeds through the lights at El Mirage during a post WWII SCTA meet.

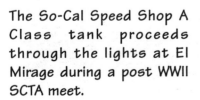

Typical of bobtail modifieds that were running on tracks around Southern California right after WWII.

DeFahrity's sharp looking pre-WWII Modified. Check the knock-off Fronty wire wheels.

This is the Tom Medley Olds V8/1949 Ford convert engine swap performed by Don Francisco in 1950. Cad and Olds engines were favorites for flathead replacements during the early '50s.

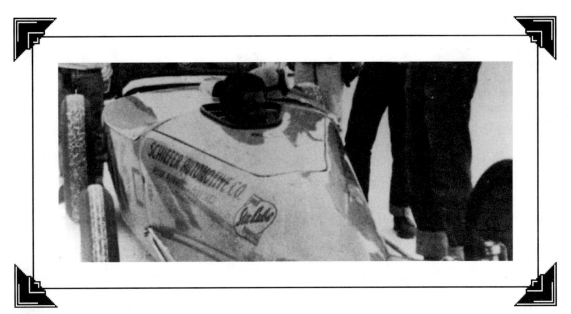

This snapshot shows how little of the driver protruded from a typical Modified Roadster, this one was from Paul Schiefer's Automotive. That trick front axle is from a pre-WW II MoPar.

HOT ROD MAGAZINE editor and National Hot Rod Association president and founder Wally Parks conceived this car in late 1956. A very spartan Plymouth, it ran big Chrysler engines and set a record of 166 mph at Daytona Beach, then turned over 180 mph at Bonneville. Ray Brock was involved, along with Dean Moon.

It was called "Suddenly…" because that was a bit of advertising Chrysler Corporation was doing at the time time, "Suddenly, it's 1960 with the forward look!"

All the hot rod efforts at early dry lakes and salt flats events were leading up to moves on major international speed records. The Summers Brothers, Bill and Bob, really got attention when their radical streamliner turned over 409 mph. This car is still around and rumored to be capable of running again, with a top speed well above the old record.

SOME REALLY EARLY LAKES STUFF

There is no information on this photo, but the '29 Ford roadster has the fenders removed (braces still in place), indicating an attempt to garner more speed at the lakes.

Earlier version of the Lakes Modified, this KPD Cragar version ran 125 mph. Note the Model A radiator shell with T bucket body. Veda Orr photo.

The objective at the lakes was to go fast. This was helped by reducing car frontal area, as with chopping and channeling. This T is radically dropped over the frame.

In the 1930's and well into the 1950's, it was common for track race cars to also run at dry lakes. Usually nothing more than a gear change was involved. This single seater was from Regg Schlemmer's speed shop out of Southgate, California.

Here's a piece of automotive history, the old sign at entrance onto the Bonneville salt flats. Utah once had pride in the flats. Jerry Jardine photo.

Anyone who has attended salt flat racing has seen this kind of maintenance being done in nearby Wendover. In earlier days, there were very few motel rooms, and testing on main street highway was common. Jerry Jardine photo.

Early racing in top speed time trials did not include a great amount of safety equipment—note this tank driver has no roll bar above the head. Current regulations are extremely stringent. Jerry Jardine photo.

It was the mid-'30s when this photo was taken, there is no identification available. The car used a narrowed Model T roadster body, the radiator / grille is from a Whippet.

No I.D. on this car either, although it is a Riley two-port engine. Many of the early modifieds used semi-elliptic front springs, Ford transverse spring and rear end.

Lots of very homemade stuff here, Franklin axle mounts atop the semi-elliptic springs to drop the car several inches (and give up axle to frame clearance), the engine is a Ford with McDowell twin plug four-port head.

Here the axle is a Chrysler unit atop the springs; a little more axle clearance available.

The chrome shop express used a beautifully detailed four-banger engine and generated more than a share of attention.

This is believed to be Willie Utzman with a flathead four-banger. The frame is not Ford, but a Ford front axle / spring has been used, along with a Ford rear end. Wheels are number 3 Buffalo.

Early frames could be narrowed quite readily by building new center and rear crossmembers. There were a large variety of grilles available.

Very unusual for the time was this highly chromed version of a single seater, running a Franklin axle with Buffalo wire wheels.

Dick Scandling of Salem, Oregon, and a couple buddies drove down to Southern California right after WW II, just to check out the hot rod scene. Like all hot rodders, they went to the various speed shops first. Here they are parked in front of the granddaddy of all shops, Bell Auto (also known as Cragar). Dick's car has a racing number on the side, an excellent way to get a ticket.

It's a '28/'29 Model A Ford roadster on stock frame, the frame covers pre-date the same ground effects skirts on modern race cars. Note the solid hood and custom grille.

This Danny Sakai modified was very typical of the narrowed single seat cars that could run both track and lakes. Veda Orr photo.

The Bob Rufi interview in this book gives a graphic description of this particular car. Originally it was the Rufi streamliner, here it was being run as the Beck Brothers streamliner. Veda Orr photo.

Typical street driven roadster at the lakes, the '29 uses a '32 grille, but the frame is Model A with fender apron still in place. Veda Orr photo.

The Model T / Model A rear spring was favored for early A rear ends, note how the Ford rear crossmember has been narrowed for the non-Ford frame. The tiny gas tank was adequate.

Blair's Speed Shop in Pasadena was one of the most famous of early hot rod emporiums in Southern California, this was the shop on Arroyo Parkway in 1948. Author Medley hung around Blair's while attending nearby Art Center, this was where his Stroker McGurk cartoons were discovered by HOT ROD MAGAZINE founder Robert Petersen.

While Scandling and his friends were at Blair's Speed Shop, Phil Weiand drove in with his 1940 Ford coupe pulling his 1927 T track roadster.

This is another scene that every hot rod visitor to Southern California grew accustomed to—hot rods on the used car lots. This nice '32 roadster was typical and average.

A hot flathead Ford V8 engine was common to most hot rods by 1948, the date of this photo. The real difference was in cubic inch displacement, with the "high dollar" boys said to have the big displacement engines. Not necessarily so.

This street '29 roadster has a one-piece hood top, mild front axle and cycle type front fenders.

One of the all-time nice street roadsters, this 1932 Ford was by Jimmy Summers and featured a stock 1936 Ford V8 engine. Never clocked, the car was radically channeled and used a V-type windshield. It sold for $2,200, which was huge money in post WW II days.

Dick Scandling in his 1932 Ford convert at the Yakima, Washington, dirt oval track. This was in 1946, when racing roadsters were often driven directly onto the track from the street.
Dick Martin photo.

Just to prove a point, here is a 1929 Model A, photographed in 1947, with an independent front suspension. A-arms on top, transverse leaf spring, probably from a Studebaker.

Dick Martin of the Washington / Oregon area had this car in 1946. It is a 1935 Ford Phaeton with a 1939 front end / bumpers / running boards. This was a relatively common conversion after WW II, but not easy to do. Dick Martin photo.

John Elfuing's A-V8 in 1946, with front end built by Tom Storey. The vertical grille is a 1942 Ford side grille. Dick Martin photo.

A 1936 Ford from Seattle showed for the "Gypsy Tour" at Long Beach, Washington, in 1945. The car had Meyers heads, four Winfield carbs. Dick Martin photo.

Bob Donker of Seattle had an A-V8 with an early model McCulloch blower for doing northwest hot rod activities in the mid-1940s. Dick Martin photo.

STUFF AT THE TRACK
(For a comprehensive look at track roadster history, see the
Tex Smith book titled ROARING ROADSTERS, by Don Radbruch.)

Early on in track roadster racing history, it was common to enter a street driven car in roundy-round events. Often the street cars were competitive. Bob VanMannen's channeled roadster was very low.

The Oka boys' famed "8-Spot" at speed on the pavement during a CRA event in the late '40s.

The Oka boys constructed this outstanding track roadster under the pepper trees in the family backyard, Yam Oka drove the brilliant red beauty. It was highly chromed and went like gangbusters. Wes Cooper photo.

Gorden Youngstrom at speed with Dick Scandling's deuce convert on the Portland Speedway—circa 1946. The car used a Thickston manifold, early V8 block; it was an example of a street driven oval track racer.

Single seaters built during the '30s were still being raced after WW II.

Pure track race cars were often based on Ford chassis components, it was common for them to run at the dry lakes. Note the block cut rear tread, used on dirt ovals.

Although many other kinds of engines were used in circle track cars, the Ford flathead V8 became the engine of choice after WW II.

HOT RODDER COMMUNICATIONS

While it is generally agreed that hot rodding has roots back to the introduction of the automobile in America, and that much of the earliest hot rodding activities were in the Midwest and eastern areas of the country, there is no doubt that the sport gained its major impetus in Southern California. Excellent year-round weather, a movie industry that focused on specialty vehicles and the presence of car-building craftsmen drove this emerging intensity. Through it all, however, no specific communications device existed to mold the hobby.

Information was mostly word-of-mouth, passed around at places where hot rod enthusiasts gathered, such as garages, cafes, and later, drive-ins. Circle track events might be heavily advertised by promoters, but grass roots hot rod events at the dry lakes were less publicized,

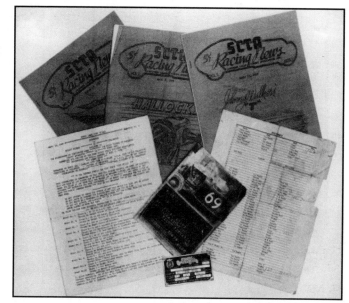

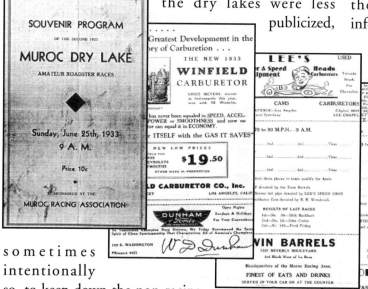

the United States, and a sort of underground information network emerged.

As racing at the dry lakes began to build during the late '20s and early '30s, there were only a few official programs published. We

sometimes intentionally so, to keep down the non-racing crowd. The first hot rod "magazine," titled *Throttle,* appeared in the late 1930s, and disappeared by World War II. *HOT ROD MAGAZINE* was not introduced until the late 1940s. Historians feel that it was the effort of Veda Orr—the only female driving member of the Southern California Timing Association—during World War II that generated much of the interest in hot rodding that would explode during the late 1940s. Veda corresponded with Southern California hot rodders who were spread around the world during the war, sending them photos and reports of what little rod action was happening. These soldiers shared the meager information with other car enthusiasts from around

include excerpts from one such program, dated June 25, 1933. Note that this event was sponsored by the Muroc Racing Association, and that it calls attention to "amateur roadster races."

Similar programs were produced in succeeding years, we show them here, but it took the information in *HOT ROD MAGAZINE* to cause the sport to explode. It also required the very real efforts of the National Hot Rod Association and a fledgling activity called drag racing to really expand the energy of hot rodding.

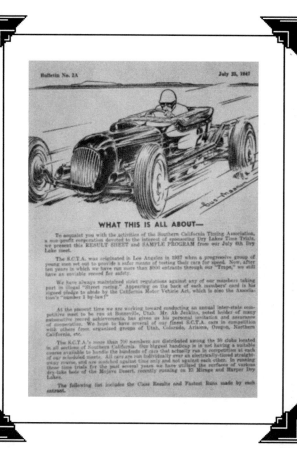

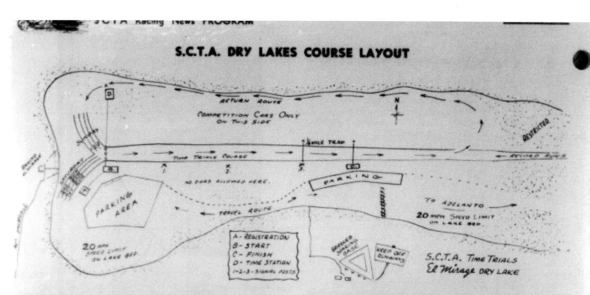

EXPLANATION.—The above illustration gives the layout on the complete running of the Two-day Meet as it affects both COMPETITION CARS and SPECTATORS. All phases of the operation, especially the running of traffic will be rigidly enforced by the PATROLS. We advise everyone to study the new layout closely and please observe the following:

1. REGISTRATION.—The Official Registration Tent and Information Booth will be located at the extreme western end of the El Mirage Dry Lake and is designated "A" on the

5. SPECTATOR TRAFFIC.—All Spectator and Non-participant Traffic will be confined to one lane of travel along the South edge of the Lake. This lane is marked continually with the old-type flags.

6. SPEED LIMIT.—A very necessary low speed limit for "Everybody" will be enforced at 20 m.p.h. at all times. This one careful observance by all cars will reduce the dust hazard to a minimum. California Highway Patrols and S.C.T.A. Mobile Patrols will enforce the 20 m.p.h. speed limit

HOT ROD ART

There is a growing acknowledgment of, and appreciation for, hot rod art, with contemporary artists coming into high demand. This is part of the general trend toward acceptance of automotive art, but as might be expected, the art of the sport has been around for decades.

We include some examples here. One of the best known of the early artists is Gus Maanum, whose work appeared in hot rodding circles everywhere. This photo is of Gus hawking art at a dry lakes meet in the late 1940s. These particular examples of Maanum art are from a book published by Bell Auto Parts and Roy Richter. In order, the drawings are of Jack Calori's roadster, Regg Schlemmer's roadster, Randy Shinn's roadster, Arnold Birner's modified, Stu Hillborn's streamliner, Bert Letner's roadster, the Johnson & Caruthers modified, Phil Remington's modified, the Burke & Francisco streamliner, Bob Rufi's streamliner, Karl Orr's modified, Bill Warth's streamliner, Danny Sakai's modified, Jack Harvey's modified and Don Blair's modified.

One of the early publishers of automotive material was Floyd Clymer. In 1949, he published a book, which had been compiled by Veda Orr, titled *Hot Rod Pictorial*. Included in this book were a few drawings by Dick Teague, an early rodder who later became famous as a new car designer in Detroit. Some of these are of the same cars that Maanum drew, but Teague's technique is quite different.

Finally, we include some art from an unknown source, submitted by Bob Stender. These are of similar cars, but they are straight side views and again, a different technique.

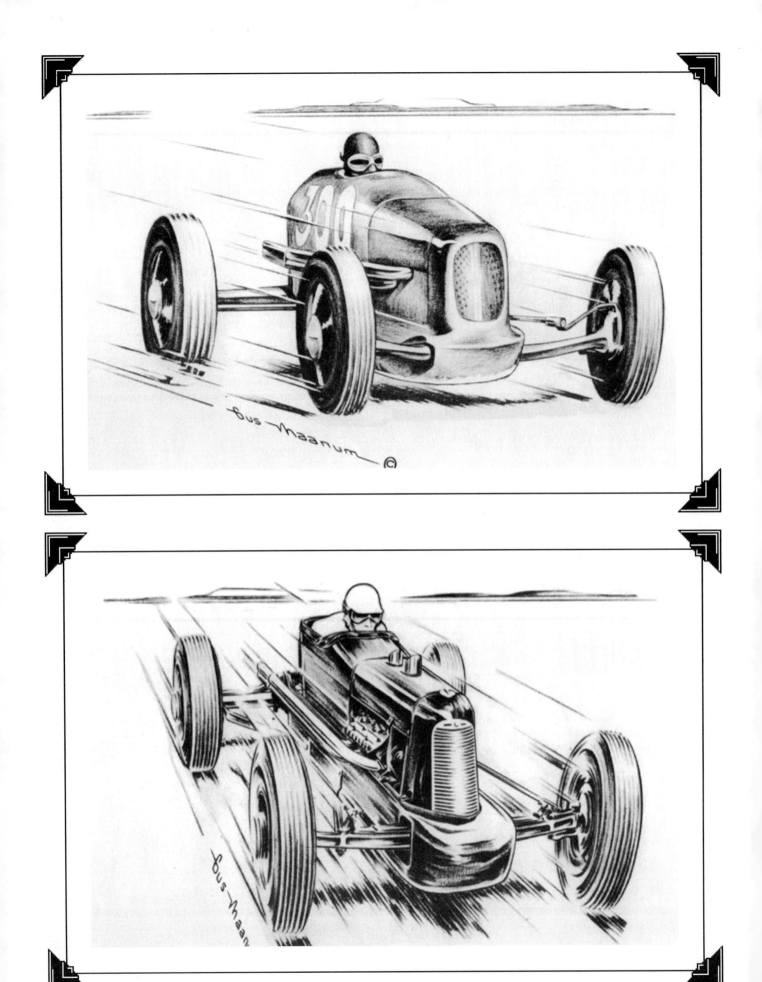

DICK TEAGUE
'47

DICK TEAGUE
'47

DICK TEAGUE
'47

DICK TEAGUE
'47

DICK TEAGUE
'47

DICK TEAGUE
'47

RICO SQUAGLIA 1923 "T" STREET ROADSTER

AKTON MILLER'S MODIFIED "T" ROADSTER

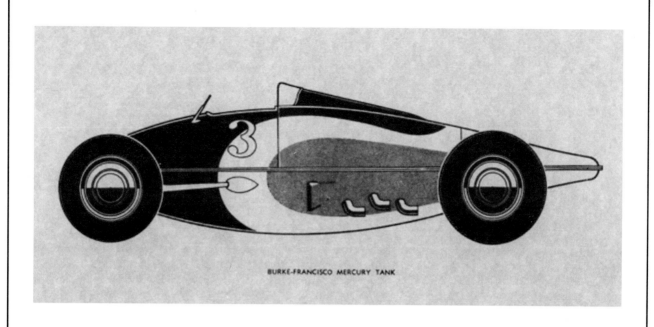

BURKE-FRANCISCO MERCURY TANK

EDDIE MILLER PONTIAC LAKESTER

PIERSON BROTHERS MODIFIED COUPE

SPAULDING BROTHERS CHEVROLET TRACK ROADSTER

THE ROLE OF CAR CLUBS

Hot rod and custom car clubs were a vital part of hot rodding as it grew into an organized hobby during the 1930s. At first, most of these clubs were formed as part of the dry lakes timing groups, and then they were formed primarily as a method of condensing points from dry lakes race cars. In some parts of the country, after World War II, clubs and associations were formed to promote circle track hot rod (roadster) racing. Then, as the National Hot Rod Association began to focus national interest on drag racing starting in 1951, clubs mushroomed across the United States and Canada. Clubs even formed in a number of other countries.

Clubs and associations were given publicity in the various car magazines and perhaps reached their zenith of popularity in the late '60s. As drag racing became more professional, and as available drag strips became fewer in number, those clubs that had been formed primarily to feature drag racing began to disappear. In their place were larger clubs and statewide associations that promoted street rod events.

One of the better known street rod clubs is the Los Angeles Roadster Club, started by Dick Scritchfield and Tex Smith. Scritchfield conceived the club idea in the mid-'50s, as the traditional type of hot rod was giving way to the newer, faster, and arguably better Detroit muscle car. This particular club gained international fame as a result of Tex's articles in *HOT ROD MAGAZINE* and articles in other car magazines. This club inspired similar groups around the country that were more interested in street driven hot rods than drag racers. Activities of the L.A. Roadster Club were touted in magazines, ultimately leading to formation of rod runs everywhere in the world.

Hot rod clubs were an offshoot of dry lakes racing in Southern California, but it didn't take them long to begin work on public image campaigns. Here, the Gripers Roadster Club perform a safety check on a Pasadena police car.

This lineup of club cars from a southeastern state illustrates the diversity most groups in the '50s and '60s enjoyed.

While early NHRA emphasis seemed to be on drag racing, it was really the local rod club and timing association that needed so much help from NHRA. To this end, the organization appeared in car shows across America, handing out free help on starting clubs, running club activities and starting drag strips.

This is an early photo of the Los Angeles Roadster Club, taken about 1962. The club was formed in 1957 to combat the rapid disappearance of traditional hot rods from Southern California streets. The club is credited with setting the foundation for the later popularity of street rods.

The Westchester Autorama of White Plains, New York, was typical of the early club-oriented shows. Most of the buildings were small, but the quality of the equipment on display was excellent.

A young Tex Smith speaks to a group of hot rodders in New Mexico concerning organizational needs and benefits of belonging to NHRA. Meetings such as this were held throughout the country, and along with the NHRA Drag/Safety Safari showing how to put on drag meets. Hot rodding flourished under this attention.

Wally Parks was an early participant at Southern California dry lakes events. He became secretary of the SCTA and in 1948 moved to Hot Rod Magazine as an editor. Shortly afterward, he joined forces with several other rodders to form the National Hot Rod Association

SHOWS AND SWAPS

Car shows have been around for decades. Most of these, however, have concentrated on new cars, and to a small extent, on antique and classic vehicles. The hot rod and custom car show can be traced to two similar events, both held in California.

Although there were a few sporadic small shows that included hot rods, customs and race cars, the first show I know of that was directed specifically at these specialty cars was the Autorama. This show was held in the Hollywood area and was sponsored by the Southern California Timing Association. Interestingly, SCTA asked a young man named Robert E. Petersen to produce the show program. Pete saw promise here, and shortly afterward launched *HOT ROD MAGAZINE*.

At almost the same time, Al Slonaker in Northern California decided to create the famous Oakland Roadster Show in the old Oakland Exposition Hall. While the SCTA show quickly disappeared into oblivion, the Oakland show continued to grow. Publicity for these events led individual rodders and rod clubs in other parts of the nation to host rod and custom shows, which teamed with drag racing to rapidly spread the enthusiasm for hot rodding.

As with every facet of hot rodding, the shows began as mere displays of street and strip equipment, but before long vehicles were created for nothing other than showing.

While specialty car shows were growing, the antique restoration part of the car hobby was quietly expanding nationwide. With this expansion came the introduction of the old car swap meet, a variation on the flea market idea. Although hot rod parts were sometimes included in these old car parts swaps, the idea of a hot rod and custom car swap didn't evolve until the early '60s. The Los Angeles Roadster Club introduced a small roadsters-only show at the Hollywood Bowl, and at the suggestion of our staff at *ROD & CUSTOM MAGAZINE*, the club rather reluctantly included a small swap meet at the third show. Both the show and the swap meet immediately outgrew the Bowl, forcing relocation to a larger facility. The swap meet expanded, magazine coverage expanded, and a few enterprising aftermarket parts people in hot rodding added displays.

These commercial exhibitors were an instant hit with rodders, so that today the largest hot rod shows and street rod runs have vendors in such quantity that no show seems "major league" without them.

Just as drag racing spun away from traditional hot rodding, so did car shows, and to some extent, street rodding.

Hot rod and custom car shows hit their stride in the late '50s and early '60s, early on they were primarily club sponsored, but they would later take on professional promoter status.

Swap meets that catered to the hot rod crowd began in earnest in the early '60s, eventually the more established old car swaps accepted the appearance of specialty performance parts as normal.

At first, car show displays were little more than wiped-clean vehicles, but participants found that additional display attention might enhance their vehicles.

Antique and classic car shows tended to be outside—often on the lawns of prestigious buildings. Car clubs found that such settings for hot rod shows worked especially well for one-day events

This was a hot rod parts supplier exhibit at one of the early L.A. Roadster Club events, a far cry from the professionalism that would come to permeate the industry.

THE EMERGENCE OF DRAG RACING

The scope of this Book Two of our HOT ROD HISTORY of necessity reaches back to the 1920s (an era we covered more fully in Book One). It also flows forward into the contemporary period as a natural progression. A part of this progression is drag racing.

Acceleration contests have been part of hot rodding from the beginning. Rarely were they under controlled conditions, most often drag races were simply street races. Usually, the street races involved only a handful of people and cars, but sometimes they were—and still are—rather intense with a large crowd.

Leaders of hot rodding in Southern California, early on, understood clearly the drastic need for organized speed contests for hot rod enthusiasts. They also recognized that the dry lakes were too remote for most of Southern California and that the rest of America needed readily accessible race sites. Happily, the United States had a ready supply of World War II military airfields in disuse, perfect places for acceleration races.

Enter the National Hot Rod Association. While there were a few abortive attempts to form drag racing

organizations, it remained for Wally Parks, then editor of *HOT ROD MAGAZINE*, to get the ball rolling in a big way. Having a direct voice to the enthusiast via the magazine was a perfect way for Parks and NHRA to lead the way. Still, it was a major undertaking, and most historians give credit to the NHRA Drag/Safety Safari tours of 1954-1955 as the catalyst needed to train groups on safe presentation of drag races.

With the increasing interest in drag racing came the first split in the hot rod sport. For awhile, most every hot rodder participated in drag racing to some degree, as well as in car shows. By the end of the '50s, however, there were some enthusiasts who preferred not to concentrate solely on racing, whether it was on a circle track, a sports car track or on a drag strip. This gave rise to street rodding, and to some extent, specializations in car shows.

We show a few of the earliest participants in drag racing. We cannot even attempt a history of drag racing—that is far too complex a subject to deal with here. Drag racing history must wait for another time, in another book.

SAN FERNANDO DRAG STRIP

Jack Mallory gets set to make a pass down the San Fernando quarter mile his home-built four-port-Riley-powered dragster. Jack's little digger ran 100-plus mph.

Tom Tolan, driver of Chuck Sawyer's blown Pontiac four-cylinder fuel dragster, pauses for the camera after another successful round.

Chuck Sawyer (left) looks on as Tom Tolan gets ready to make another pass down the San Fernando strip.

Chuck Sawyer (foreground) talks things over with Tic Vertrees as he makes final adjustments to the fuel system. Driver Tom Tolan checks the chute.

LIONS DRAG STRIP

The world's fastest four-cylinder dragster in the '60s is hazing the hard rubber slicks at Lions Drag Strip. Chuck Sawyer's 4-71 huffed Pontiac four banger ran a best of 171.75 mph.

POMONA DRAG STRIP

A modified roadster smokes the tires off the Pomona Drag Strip starting line. Note the elaborate starting line stand and the redundant safety equipment; two fire extinguishers!

No question about the lakes heritage of this slammed coupe. Whether or not a huge reduction in frontal area helped early drag cars is debatable, but it did make them look fast!

Dempsey Wilson Cams sponsored this flathead-powered dragster. Stripped of everything but the bare essentials, early "rail jobs" like this were the forerunners of today's dragsters.

While the flathead still reigned supreme in the early '50s, overhead equipped cars like this Cadillac-powered T roadster, were beginning to appear. This particular car, owner unknown, features a three carb manifold.

The team of Winfield and Fisher ran this six-cylinder three-window Deuce coupe. The evolution of a street-driven hot rod to a race-only machine was a short and sweet affair.

This classic '32 Ford highboy roadster ran at Santa Ana drags in the early '50s. Check out the unique wide louvers in the hood side panels.

This was obviously a street-driven Model A roadster, shorn of radiator for the sake of drag racing. Big and bigger engines were the quick way to performance.

Four-cylinder engines were still running at the dry lakes, and they could be fairly competitive at the early drags.

Rear-engined cars were not uncommon at the lakes, and they showed at the drags as well.

The Saugus drag site was north of Los Angeles, an area now totally covered by urban sprawl. During the early '50s, when these photos were taken, the desert held sway. These are two typical street warriors of the day.

The Ford inline six-cylinder had a reputation for scattering parts when hopped up, yet it could be made into a potent performer in track roadsters. This is a typical street version running at the drags.

Hot rodders had long since learned that power-to-weight ratios are all important in basic acceleration, which led to some very early experiments with what came to be called Rail Jobs. This example was very nicely constructed.

A Hollywood Graham takes on a hot 1940 Ford coupe at Saugus, this type of stock-bodied matchup was very popular.

Stock-bodied Chevy's didn't always match up to the hot flathead V8 Fords, but they could be made to run. With correct pipes, they make a dynamite sound!

Chances are very good that this late-model Ford sedan was pulled the entire distance by the hopped-up pickup.

THE EVOLUTION OF THE DRAGS

The rear-engined style dragster was a spillover from the dry lakes, and it did not prove particularly successful at the early drags.

By the time drag racing had evolved into this configuration for the ultimate dragsters of the

The Ford flathead V8 engine was highly evolved by the time drag racing got going good in the early '50s. Even with a huge set-back in the chassis, though, it was not a real match for the new breed of overhead valve V8 engines.

'60s, this part of hot rodding had taken on an entirely new direction.